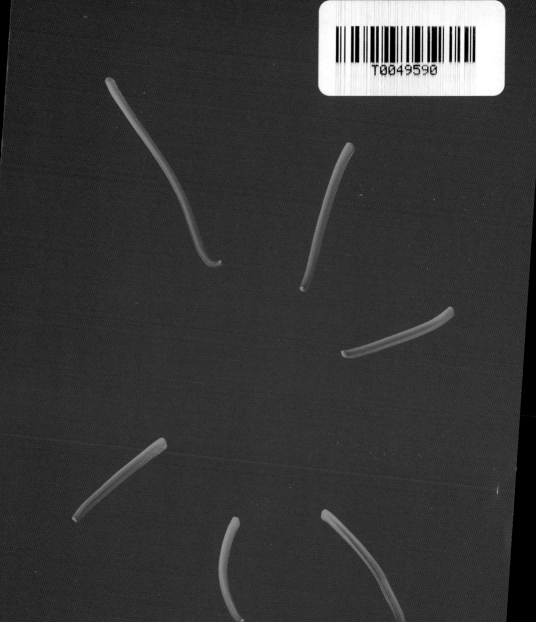

PRIMITIVE
CAMPING
& BUSHCRAFT

A Step-by-Step Guide to Surviving and Thriving in the Great Outdoors

CHRIS SPEIR

FOREWORD

Hey there, fellow adventurers and outdoor enthusiasts! Ever feel the call of the wild, the urge to step beyond the boundaries of the modern world and into the untamed embrace of nature? If you've got that itch, this book is your ultimate guide to scratching it. Grab a seat by the campfire because we're diving into the exhilarating world of primitive camping and bushcraft.

But first, let me introduce myself: I'm Jake Trent, the owner/operator of Buckeye Bushcraft LLC. My journey began back in 2009 when I first learned the ropes (literally!) from my old man. Since then, I've been lucky enough to teach wilderness skills and survival as my full-time job, work as an instructor at the Pathfinder School, become Wilderness First Aid certified by the Red Cross and get my ham radio operator license (which is like having a lifeline when you're in the middle of nowhere).

Here's the scoop on why this book is like no other. Author Chris Speir digs into three crucial elements: bushcraft, primitive camping and wilderness skills. Think of it as a triple-threat survival package. Bushcraft is the art of thriving in the wild using age-old techniques. Primitive camping adds the modern twists that help us adapt those techniques to our ever-changing world. And wilderness skills mixes all areas of the outdoors, including trapping, hunting, fire-making, shelter building and more.

Horace Kephart once said, "The man who goes afoot, prepared to camp anywhere and in any weather, is the most independent fellow on earth." Knowing how to light a fire, build a shelter, find clean water—these timeless skills are the backbone of self-reliance. Folks today generally don't get outdoors enough, and the art forms of primitive camping, bushcraft and wilderness skills are dying as a result. But thanks to Chris and his expertise, this book will pass on knowledge to others starting down this long, incredible road of learning new skills that are more valuable than some might think!

So, if you're ready to trade your cubicle for a canopy of trees, your keyboard for a knife and your Wi-Fi for wide-open spaces, this book is your ticket. Here's to you, the wild and the journey ahead!

Cheers,

JAKE TRENT

buckeyebushcraft.com

CONTENTS

What Is
PRIMITIVE
CAMPING?

When it comes to primitive camping, bushcraft and survival, there really is no wrong approach—as long as you're thinking outside the box, you'll find there are several ways to accomplish a particular task. You do not have to have the latest gear or the most expensive knife to have a great time. The main goal of primitive camping is to enjoy the company of the ones you are with, reconnect with nature, clear your mind and have fun.

Some may ask, "Why would you want to live in the woods?" or "Why would you want to subject yourself to miserable conditions?" Well, in a technology-dependent world, the great outdoors is a beautiful place to unplug from your fast-paced daily life. It allows you to recharge your internal batteries and offers peace, quiet and nothing but your thoughts. What's not to love about that? OK—maybe the heat, the cold or the rain (or in my neck of the woods, the mosquitoes) might keep you from fully enjoying yourself. But misery is often a choice, and you can choose to see the positive side of enduring some discomforts to enjoy the beautiful natural world God created. For me personally, the great outdoors is the perfect place to catch up on reading my Bible, praying and maintaining my

Sticks found around camp can be carved into extra tent stakes or fire roasting spits or set aside to use as fire fuel.

spiritual peace of mind. Psalm 145:5 says, "On the glorious splendor of your majesty, and on your wondrous works, I will meditate." What better place to meditate than in the wilderness of God's creation?

Primitive camping is rooted in our ancient history. The men and women who inhabited our planet before us lived off the grid by default and thrived using only what was available to them. They worked hard for their food, and they did it without modern-day conveniences like electricity, running water, a flushable toilet and central air and heat. Pioneers and explorers throughout history depended on their knowledge of the great outdoors; they knew how to use it to their advantage.

BUSHCRAFT AND SURVIVAL

You may have heard of bushcraft and survival and wondered why they have become so popular in recent years. Survival schools and bushcraft courses are popping up everywhere, and the two disciplines have turned into a multi-million dollar industry. Nearly 4 million Americans now classify themselves as survivalists or bushcrafters, and many have managed to transform those hobbies into a lifestyle. Major television networks have naturally been cashing in on the trend through popular shows such as *Survivor*, *Naked and Afraid* and *Alone*, to name a few. These TV shows stir interest and give viewers a window into a simplistic life in the wild without leaving the comfort of their couch, allowing them to get a taste of the experience without the consequences of making wrong choices or subjecting themselves to harsh environments.

But even with its growing popularity, many people still don't know what bushcraft is. Put simply, bushcraft is the skill required to live in the woods or a natural setting for a prolonged period without relying on modern conveniences, using nature to make or acquire everything needed to survive. It is truly an art form—one that encourages creativity and builds problem-solving and improvisational skills to get what you need.

So, how does bushcraft differ from survival? Survival is an emergency situation in which the goal is to keep yourself alive and return to civilization's safety. Survival is typically a 72-hour timeframe after a man-made or natural disaster, accident or medical emergency that occurred away from civilization. Bushcraft is the opposite, in the sense that you intentionally leave society to survive and thrive in the wild.

A clearer understanding of what defines bushcraft leads us to a fundamental question: How does bushcraft differ from primitive camping? I have thought long and hard about this one. Yes, primitive camping and bushcraft are very closely related, and some influential people in the field will even argue they are synonymous. To me, primitive camping allows you to bring more modern conveniences to enjoy your camping trip—but even if you do so, there will always be plenty you can't pack, at which point you'll need to rely on nature. That's where bushcraft comes in; the two concepts truly work in tandem.

For instance, I find a hammock very comfortable to sleep in. It's always

It's never too early to start building a connection with the great outdoors.

the cooler option in the summer, and with an underquilt and wool blanket, depending on the environment, it can also be comfortable during winter. Making a bed from sticks and tree branches is not my idea of a good night's sleep. Of course, you could rake up a bunch of leaves to use as a mattress, but in south Mississippi during the summer, insects are guaranteed to crawl on you all night. Don't get me wrong, I have spent time in the dirt on many camping trips and even slept without shelter. But with primitive camping, even a cheap hammock or tent is preferred. Think of primitive camping as the gateway to bushcraft and survival. I know how to make shelter in a natural environment

and make rope from grass and tree bark. I can start a fire half a dozen different ways. I have trained in many aspects of bushcraft and survival but still prefer a good ole Bic lighter, freeze-dried dinners, a hammock and a solar lantern.

Many people will argue with me on this point, but what some consider to be "survival" and "bushcraft" is really just primitive camping. The version of primitive camping detailed in the following pages includes several bushcraft and survival techniques intended to create the best outdoor experience possible. It is meant to be enjoyed by anyone who wants to have a relaxing and rewarding connection with God's beautiful creation.

WHAT TO KNOW BEFORE YOU GO

If you've decided primitive camping is right for you, you'll want to familiarize yourself with these concepts before your first big adventure into the woods.

FIRST AID

I AM A RETIRED United States Air Force medic, where I was a Nationally Registered EMT. I have trained thousands of brand-new medics for their military careers and have extensive training in basic and advanced life support spanning 20 years of service. I was deployed numerous times and responded to and treated more injuries than I can remember. So, naturally, I believe one of the most essential items for any outdoor adventure is a first aid kit. First aid is a very in-depth subject; I will not cover how to use every item in the first aid kit, nor will I go over various injuries and diseases. Instead, I will give you a guide to building your own basic first aid kit and encourage you to study wilderness first aid or, at minimum, know basic life support measures before embarking on hiking or camping trips. There are hundreds of excellent resources out there that can make you proficient in first aid in a wilderness setting. The items listed in this section are what I typically carry in my kit, but I am not a doctor and cannot give you medical advice. I can merely explain how I assemble and use my kit.

A first aid kit for camping should not only anticipate the types of injuries that can occur in the wild, it should also be equipped to handle the reality that you cannot make it back to more advanced medical care quickly. A typical primitive camping trip for me is at least a 5-mile trek into the woods, which means help may take a long time to arrive in an emergency. When it comes to treating injuries, you will

SAFETY VESTS

Hunting accidents are not commonplace in the United States, but they do happen. It is possible to be camping deep in the woods during specific hunting seasons and be misidentified as a large game animal and accidentally shot. Bright orange safety vests are highly recommended if you intend to camp on public lands during hunting season.

A red bag makes your first aid kit easy for you and others to recognize.

probably end up using a first aid kit on someone other than yourself, but you should also be ready to care for yourself if you plan to camp alone. The most common injuries on camping trips are cuts, burns, splinters, blisters and strains, but you should also prepare for the more severe types of injuries you could sustain in the woods, such as broken bones, gunshot wounds and severed limbs.

Many of the items on the following pages can and should be used for more than one type of injury. It is always wise to carry things that serve more than one purpose, as will be discussed more in the Gear section (pg. 40). This is not an exhaustive list of everything needed to treat every possible camping injury but rather a recommendation to follow in order to treat various trauma and medical emergencies in the field until you can reach more definitive medical care or more definitive care can reach you. Some premade kits will contain many of the same items, but I built this kit based on my background and preferences. This kit allows me to treat both myself and others and is relatively compact and easy to carry in my backpack.

OVER-THE-COUNTER MEDICINES

Being miles away from medical attention is not where you want to find out you are allergic to something, which is why you should always bring diphenhydramine (Benadryl) and famotidine or ranitidine (Zantac), which are very effective at treating allergic reactions you may encounter in the wilderness. Benadryl is also very effective at treating nausea, vomiting and dizziness, while Zantac is excellent for heartburn or indigestion. Acetaminophen and ibuprofen are good for aches, pains and fever, all of which can easily occur on a long camping trip.

SUPERGLUE

While some people may associate it with arts and crafts, superglue can be used to treat fairly severe cuts. During the Vietnam War, combat medics used superglue on the battlefield. Back then, it came in a spray can that allowed the medic to spray the glue directly on the wound, and today it comes in a small tube, which is easier to apply. In emergency rooms around the country, lacerations that need to be closed but don't require sutures are sealed with medical-grade superglue. This glue lasts for several days and starts to peel away naturally due to the oils on your skin, making it a convenient alternative to getting sutures removed. I have used superglue for minor cuts for years. With any cut, make sure it is adequately cleaned with water and alcohol before gluing.

TAMPONS

Tampons can be unfolded and wrapped with elastic gauze to form a makeshift pressure dressing. However, I do not recommend inserting a tampon into an open wound. Whether or not the tampon was created for bullet wounds is an endless debate between untrained individuals and the medical community—but the absolute truth is a tampon cannot absorb enough blood to help with clotting, which means it could possibly cause even more bleeding. So, the most effective way to use one is to layer it under gauze or cotton cloth and apply pressure. Beyond its intended use and its utility in a first aid kit, a tampon can also be used to start a friction fire (pg. 163).

ALCOHOLS

Not only can you kill 99.99 percent of the germs on your hands with ordinary hand sanitizer, you can also use it to create fire. The same goes for alcohol pads. An alcohol pad ignites via spark very quickly and burns longer due to the cotton pad. Iodine can clean your cuts as well as disinfect your drinking water, which you can read more about on pg. 118.

DUCT TAPE

Duct tape exists in a world of its own (the TV show *MythBusters* devoted many episodes to showing us how handy this adhesive truly is). You can use duct tape for splinting a sprained, strained or fractured limb by lining your leg or arm with a stick and wrapping it around to immobilize the extremity. You can also use duct tape to close a wound, cover and waterproof an injury or even repair clothing and tents. There are more uses for duct tape than can be effectively described in a single book—the possibilities are endless, as long as you use your imagination.

THE ABCS OF FIRST AID

To simplify first aid, you need to remember your ABCs:

Airway
Breathing
Circulation

This little mnemonic will help you remember the steps to take in any first aid situation. First, always check the airway. If a person requiring first aid is sporadically breathing or speaking to you, the airway is clear. Next, check the breathing. If the chest is rising and falling or the subject is talking, then they are breathing. Circulation can be assessed by bleeding or whether the heart has stopped pumping. If the heart stops pumping, the subject will not be breathing and will have to tilt their head back to open the airway. Hopefully, you have taken a CPR class and are familiar with administering oxygen and chest compressions (if not, look into this ASAP). If the subject is

KIT BAG

To carry all of these first aid items, I purchased a small but roomy bag with dual zippers at Dollar General. I chose red because it's highly visible outdoors, but a first aid kit does not necessarily have to be in a red bag. You can also make yours as small or as large as you want as long as you feel comfortable carrying it. At the bare minimum, purchase a premade kit online or at a sporting goods store before you head to the woods. I have made a shopping list of these items on my Amazon influencer page available at *amazon.com/shop/ speiroutdoors*.

talking and breathing, look for active bleeding; if found, cover the wound in gauze, apply pressure and raise the limb above the heart if possible. It's likely you have instinctively used this ABC method before in an emergency without even realizing it. It is always good to know, not just for camping or outdoor activities but for daily life, especially if you have children or elderly family members.

If you can't fit everything into the kit, bring as many multi-purpose items as you can.

FIRST AID KIT CHECKLIST

☐ Pressure bandages
☐ Compressed gauze
☐ Tourniquet
☐ Hemostats
☐ Hemostatic wound dressing (contains a clotting agent to stop bleeding)
☐ Suture material (needle and thread at a minimum)
☐ Superglue
☐ Gauze bandage
☐ Triple antibiotic ointment
☐ Water-based gel-saturated gauze
☐ Triangular bandage
☐ Elastic bandages
☐ Waterproof medical tape
☐ Splinting material (SAM Splint)
☐ Adhesive bandages
☐ Gauze pads
☐ Gauze rolls
☐ Butterfly bandages
☐ Moleskin
☐ Duct tape
☐ Tampons
☐ Feminine napkins or pads
☐ Magnifying glass
☐ Tweezers
☐ Chapstick
☐ Sanitary wipes
☐ Hand sanitizer
☐ Alcohol pads
☐ Iodine solution
☐ Acetaminophen (Tylenol)
☐ Ibuprofen (Motrin)
☐ Diphenhydramine (Benadryl)
☐ Famotidine or Ranitidine (Zantac)

FINDING THE RIGHT KNIFE

THE SINGLE MOST IMPORTANT tool you can take with you into the woods, aside from a metal container (pg. 60), is a good quality sheath or belt knife. And perhaps the second most important tool you can pack is a backup knife—you always want to have more than one knife in the event that you break or lose one. Your knife will easily become your most used tool on any trip, from cleaning fish and wild game to splitting firewood and starting fires. A good quality knife can even cut down small trees and carve any camping utensils you conjure up.

TYPES OF STEEL

When selecting your knife, there are two common types of metal you'll see: stainless steel and high-carbon steel. Without turning this into a chemistry class, all steel has some degree of carbon in the makeup to make it stronger, but the main difference is stainless steel is more malleable and less brittle than carbon steel. Stainless steel has a metallic element called chromium added to it that gives it its anti-corrosive and tarnish-resistant finish, resulting in that highly polished shine. High-carbon steel knives are more rigid and robust but more brittle and prone to chipping and cracking, especially in colder weather. They are also more rust-prone and do not hold an edge as long as stainless steel knives. So why would you select a carbon steel knife? High carbon steel is superior at starting fires with a ferrocerium rod (ferro rod) and less prone to blade warping when using a mallet to baton through wood (pg. 21) or cutting small trees.

TANG

Your knife will go through tons of abuse while primitive camping, so when making a selection, you want to consider the tang of the knife.

The tang is the part of the knife blade that extends into the handle. There are wide varieties of knife tangs, but we will concentrate on just two of the most common types, the full tang and

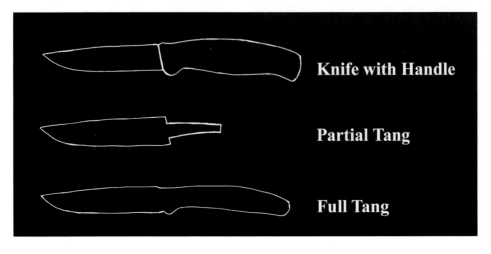

Knife with Handle

Partial Tang

Full Tang

the partial tang. A partial tang does not run through the entire handle, which makes the knife comparatively weaker and subject to breakage—especially when using your knife to split firewood or for other very demanding tasks. But they tend to be less expensive than full tang knives. A full tang runs all the way through the handle. The handle is made of two halves called scales, which are affixed to the tang, making the full tang knife much stronger and able to withstand much more abuse than a partial tang knife.

GRIND

Another important consideration when choosing your knife is the type of grind. The grind refers to how the knife blade's edge is ground down to make a razor-sharp edge for cutting. Many people tend to only consider the tang and overlook the grind, but a good grind is necessary for various common tasks. Let's explore the four grinds most often used by primitive campers.

The Scandinavian or Scandi and the flat grind are the most common blade grinds for bushcrafters and primitive campers. They are very easily sharpened and great for carving and woodworking.

A hollow grind offers a sharp and precise cut ideal for delicate tasks but the blade may be susceptible to damage with heavy-duty use. Conversely, with its outwardly curved blade edge formed by continuous tapering, a convex grind provides a robust and durable edge suitable for demanding tasks. Still, it may lack the precision and sharpness of other grinds. The hollow grind and convex grind can be more challenging to sharpen due to their curved bevels, which require more skill to maintain the correct angle during sharpening.

SPINE

Another important aspect of knife selection is ensuring your knife has a sharp 90-degree spine. Many new flashy knives marketed as being specifically for bushcraft or survival

PREVENTING RUST

Many high-carbon steel knives now come with a powder coating to prevent rusting, but you do not need a powder coating on your knife blade to maintain it. This coating simply makes the knife look better and more "tactical." In fact, powder coating is often not conducive to some of the tasks you'll be performing on camping trips. In my outdoor videos, I always use the catchphrase "You're going to use your trusty but not rusty knife." Maintaining your knife in the field is easy—to keep it from rusting, just keep it dry and apply a small amount of oil to the blade after daily use.

have stylistic ridges on the spine that often serve no purpose other than looking pretty. These ridges hinder you from using the spine of your blade to strike a ferro rod or making fine shavings for tinder.

SHARPENER

When it comes to knife sharpening, there are so many different options, including sharpening stones, diamond plates, ceramic sharpeners and even leather belts that can be used to maintain the edge of your blade (one of the primary reasons I always wear a leather belt in the field, in addition to using it to hold up my pants or haul firewood). Leather will not sharpen the blade but it will allow the blade to hold an edge longer. This method is called stropping. Stropping a knife involves running the blade along a leather strap (or strop, or belt) in a reverse cutting motion to align the microscopic teeth of the blade edge. This process polishes the edge, removes any burrs and refines the sharpness, resulting in a smoother, more efficient cut and prolonged sharpness. A smooth stone from a creek or stream can sharpen your knife, and then you can use your leather belt to make it razor-sharp.

Many knife sharpeners come with angle guides to ensure you hold your knife at the correct angle. I highly recommend the Benchmade Guided Field Sharpener—it revolutionized sharpening for me and helped me realize that I had been doing it incorrectly from the beginning. It has 20-degree guides with a coarse side, smooth side, ceramic side and leather stropping side. It can be found on my Amazon influencer page.

LENGTH

Ideal knife length depends on your intended use for it. Personally, I have found between 4 and 5 inches is the perfect length for a primitive camping knife blade as it allows you to process firewood. The blade should be relatively thick, usually between 3/32 and 3/16 of an inch. The thicker the blade, the more abuse it will be able to withstand, especially when splitting firewood. Some bushcrafters and survivalists frown upon using your knife to split wood, but sometimes it's the best option available. Of course, this will put a lot of stress on your knife and you'll have to sharpen your blade more often.

I carry my primary knife, the Morakniv Garberg or BPS Bushcraft 2, and I also have a backup knife, the Morakniv Companion HD. These knives are great, but the Garberg or Bushcraft 2 are the ones I use to split firewood. Its blade is also perfect for splitting small logs.

BATONING

Batoning involves splitting wood into halves with the use of a mallet. To make a mallet, simply carve a handle into a large piece of wood (your mallet doesn't necessarily have to have a handle, but if it's a larger piece of wood, it will be easier to hold). To split the wood, place your knife at the top of the flat side of the log so the blade protrudes on the other side. Split the log by using your mallet to hammer the knife through the length of the wood or log. You can also use your mallet and knife to cut down a 2-inch-thick sapling tree by using the same concept.

BASIC SKILLS

Before heading out on your first primitive camping adventure,
you need at least a basic understanding of a few essential skills:

- HOW TO USE A COMPASS
- HOW TO READ A MAP
- HOW TO TIE A FEW COMMON KNOTS
- CAMP SAFETY
- HOW TO PROPERLY DISPOSE OF HUMAN WASTE

Keep your compass on a lanyard or necklace to avoid losing it.

In all your ways acknowledge Him, and He shall direct your path. Proverbs 3:6

COMPASS

THE COMPASS HAS seen various upgrades in the nearly 2,000 years since it was created, but its function has remained the same: to point you in the right direction. You do not necessarily need a compass on simple trips outdoors, but this tool is invaluable if you are looking to travel with a map over long distances. And in today's tech-heavy world, a compass stands out for its simplicity—it doesn't rely on batteries or GPS satellites that can malfunction or go offline and you

don't have to upgrade the firmware! You can use a compass with or without a map, but using both will yield the best results, particularly if you are traveling in an area you have never been to before. Regardless of which type of compass you have, it will always have a travel arrow, orientation arrow, magnetized needle and azimuth ring. Some also have mirrors and sights to help with bearings and scales when map reading.

Ethan Shaw's article "How To Use a Compass: The Ultimate Guide to Navigation" in *Outdoors Generations* is a great additional resource.

❶ MAGNETIZED NEEDLE

When you hold a compass in your hand and turn your body left or right, this red or brightly colored needle will always point toward magnetic north (unless there are magnets near the compass). Magnetic north is not true north, which is Earth's North Pole. So, you may ask yourself, "What good is a compass if it doesn't point to true north?" The difference between true north and magnetic north is called magnetic declination, and this is where the orienting arrow will come into play (see below). Today, every map is drawn using the North Pole as true north while the legend features a declination diagram, which shows the direction of true north with a star and another line showing magnetic north with "MN" or another designation. Use this diagram to set your compass to true north. Magnetic north moves over time as the magnetic poles move back and forth, so to avoid getting lost while using your map and compass to travel long distances, use a current map.

❷ ORIENTING ARROW

The orienting arrow shows you where magnetic north is in relation to true north and is used to orient your compass. When you set up your compass, you'll turn the orienting arrow until it fits around the magnetized needle to "box" the needle.

❸ TRAVEL ARROW

Found on the front of your compass, this arrow shows you the direction you are traveling. Different brands use different styles of travel arrows, but they all work similarly by pointing in the direction you will walk.

BEARING

When traveling with a compass, you want to take a "bearing," which is a path of travel between two points using a landmark on the map or in your line of sight. Hold your compass level in front of you and look in your direction of travel. If a tree (or some other terrestrial object in the distance) is in your line of sight, walk to that tree, then make another bearing and repeat the process until you have reached your intended destination on the map.

❹ AZIMUTH RING

This is the ring around the compass with measurements ranging from 0 to 360 degrees. On most modern compasses, this ring freely turns and allows you to "box" the needle and take a bearing simultaneously. Depending on the compass, the azimuth ring will have some indicator or "bearing line" indicating the direction of travel.

PUTTING IT ALL TOGETHER

To use your compass in conjunction with your map, place the compass on the map with the edge of the tool on the true northline. Rotate your map and compass until the red arrow inside the compass is pointed toward the magnetic northline.

Box your arrow by turning the azimuth ring until the red arrow is inside the needle outline inside the compass. Rotate both the map and compass until the red needle is inside the box; now you are pointing in the right direction. Your map and compass are now oriented to true north, and you can use the travel arrow to show you which direction you are heading.

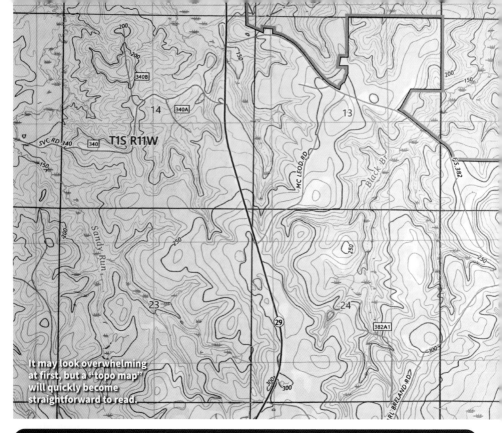

It may look overwhelming at first, but a "topo map" will quickly become straightforward to read.

TOPOGRAPHICAL MAP

GROWING UP, I DIDN'T have GPS; I had a Rand McNally road atlas! Any time my family took a road trip, we would have to open the atlas to whatever state we were driving through, review the path on the map and follow the signs on the highway. Using the map and signs together always led us to our destination. A map of the area you will be camping and hiking in is a useful tool that will help you identify where you are and guide you to where you want to go.

Today's outdoor maps are typically topographic maps based off of the United States Geological Survey (USGS). You can download and print practically any topographic map of the United States at: *ngmdb.usgs. gov/topoview/viewer/*. According to the USGS website: "The distinctive characteristic of a topographic map is the use of elevation contour lines to show the shape of the Earth's surface. Elevation contours are imaginary lines connecting points having the same elevation on the surface of the land above or below a reference surface, which is usually mean sea level. Contours make it possible to show the height and shape of mountains, the depths of the ocean bottom, and the steepness of slopes.

USGS topographic maps also show many other kinds of geographic features, including roads, railroads, rivers, streams, lakes, boundaries, place or feature names, mountains, and much more. Older maps (published before 2006) show additional features such as trails, buildings, towns, mountain elevations, and survey control points.

these two index lines. Depending on the scale and brand of your map, the contour lines will have an interval of 10 to 80 feet between them. USGS maps typically have 10-foot contour intervals, meaning each contour line is 10 feet higher or lower than the previous one.

LEGEND
Every map company uses different symbols on the legend. The downloadable USGS maps have a separate printable page for the legend (note that these maps only include road classifications). Make sure you print the legend and familiarize yourself with it before you head out.

SCALE
The map's scale is determined by the publisher. If you look to the bottom of the map, it will typically have a ratio of either 1:24000 or 1:26000 (some maps may vary). The 1 in this ratio is 1 inch, meaning that 1 inch on the map is equivalent to 24,000 inches in real life. Larger-scale maps show less detail than smaller-scale maps—the smaller the scale, the better idea of the terrain. Usually, the scale is at the bottom center of the map, and it includes a line with miles and feet or kilometers and meters. This scale helps you determine the distance on the map. Use the edge of your compass or a piece of string with this scale to determine the distance you need to travel. I have seen people place a length of string on the map to follow riverbeds or contour lines on their map then stretch this string along the map scale for a very accurate distance for travel.

Those will be added to more current maps over time."

CONTOUR LINES
Topographic maps show how a 3D landscape looks on 2D paper using contour lines. Contour lines show how the terrain looks from a top-down perspective. When the lines are close together, the landscape is steep; when they are farther apart, it's a gradual slope. As you look at the map, you will naturally visualize the terrain in a 3D perspective. Every fifth contour line is darker and thicker than the others and is called an index line, and there is a number on this line that designates the elevation change. If you were to draw a line on the map in the direction you want to travel, and one index line says 200 and the next says 150, you know you'll be traveling downhill because your elevation drops 50 feet between

KNOTS

OVER THE YEARS, I have tied nearly every knot you can find in a given outdoors book. I've used various knots to secure, lash and tie down everything from heavy loads on a vehicle to a simple loop used to hang a pot over a fire. Knowing how to tie specific knots or loops on a primitive camping trip is invaluable, and in my experience, I have found there are nine knots that are particularly helpful.

NOTE: I use the word "knot" collectively when tying or securing anything. Knots, loops and hitches are technically different, but to avoid confusion, I will use "knot" going forward.

TERMS TO KNOW IN INSTRUCTIONS

Standing end The end of the rope that has been tied off or is not used to tie the knot.
Working end The long end of the rope you are working with.
Standing part The part of the rope that is in between the standing end and working end.
Bight A curvature of the cordage where both working and standing ends come in contact with each other. For example, the overhand loop knot or "loop on a bight."

LARK'S HEAD OR COW HITCH

This knot is straightforward and does not usually jam up. It's used to hang gear and add loops and tie-offs and is frequently paired with a toggle.

Step 1 Double over your cordage and place it behind or through the object you want to secure.
Step 2 Pass the working end of your cordage through the eye or bight.
Step 3 Pull tight.

CLOVE HITCH ▼

This knot is one of the most common knots for outdoor tasks. You will use this knot to secure your cordage to anything. It's easy to tie and untie.

Step 1 Loop your cordage around your object to make a single hitch, then bring the working end around the object again.
Step 2 Bring the working end underneath itself.
Step 3 Pull tight.

▲ GUNNER'S KNOT OR CONSTRICTOR KNOT

This knot is closely related to the clove hitch and is exceptionally secure. It's characterized as a binding knot and is rather impossible to untie once a heavy load has been put on it—one of the only ways to undo this knot is to cut it.

Step 1 Make a loose clove hitch.
Step 2 Tuck the standing end under the working end.
Step 3 Pull tight.

PRUSIK KNOT

From catfishing to ridgelines, this little knot can stay securely in place when under a heavy load, but you can move it freely up and down as needed. You can secure any tarp or shelter in just a few minutes by making a few loops from some cordage. Usually, this knot will be made onto another rope, such as a ridgeline for a shelter (pg. 87).

Step 1 Make a loop or bight in your cordage and pass it on the backside of the rope you wish to tie it onto. Then pass the remainder through the loop.
Step 2 Loop it around your rope again and back through the loop.
Step 3 Loop it around and back through the loop one more time.
Step 4 Pull the rope tight. The knot should look like a fist with a loop hanging from the bottom.

ARBOR KNOT ▼

Also called the Canadian jam knot or bushcraft zip tie, this knot has multiple outdoor uses, from securing a load to making handles for a bucksaw. Most often, it's used to secure fishing line to a reel.

Step 1 Make an overhand knot (stopper knot) on the end of your cordage.
Step 2 Loop your working end around the object.
Step 3 Make another overhand knot around the standing end of the cordage.
Step 4 Pull tight.

▲ OVERHAND LOOP KNOT

The overhand loop knot is the easiest to learn and most likely to be used. It's used to make ridgelines, secure tarps with a toggle, secure pots when cooking with a tripod and more. This is often a permanent knot in the end of your cordage after a heavy load has been applied. If you do not want or need a permanent knot, use a bowline knot (pg. 33).

Step 1 Double your rope over on one end, making a loop or bight.
Step 2 Simply tie a knot with the double cordage adjusting for the size loop you require.
Step 3 Pull tight.

BUNTLINE HITCH ▼

This hitch holds exceptionally well, especially when used to tighten your guyline for your shelter (pg. 96).

Step 1 Place your cordage around a fixed object and cross the rope's standing end to complete what's known as a "crossing turn."
Step 2 Bring the working end underneath the standing end and pull. This will create a half knot, essentially making what is called a "friction noose," which is excellent for guylines.
Step 3 Pull tight.

▲ MARLINSPIKE HITCH

With more uses than can be listed here, this hitch is exceptionally sound for hanging pots from a tripod or gear from a tree. It is used with a stick or toggle to create a handle when you have a thin string or cordage that could cut your hands.

Step 1 Make a loop with your cordage. The working end should be under the standing end.
Step 2 Your cordage should resemble a pretzel shape.
Step 3 Put your toggle or "spike" into the middle of the pretzel shape.
Step 4 Pull tight.

BOWLINE KNOT OR LOOP

This knot is often memorized via the phrase, "The rabbit comes out of the hole and around the tree. Then back into the hole." The bowline is a fixed-size loop, and there are several variations. You will use this knot for everything from securing gear to tightening guylines and ridgelines to making a pot hanger for a cooking tripod (pg. 238).

Step 1 Make a counterclockwise overhand loop.
Step 2 Bring your working end through the back side of the loop.
Step 3 Bring the working end around the standing end above the loop.
Step 4 Bring the working end around and down through the loop.
Step 5 Pull tight.

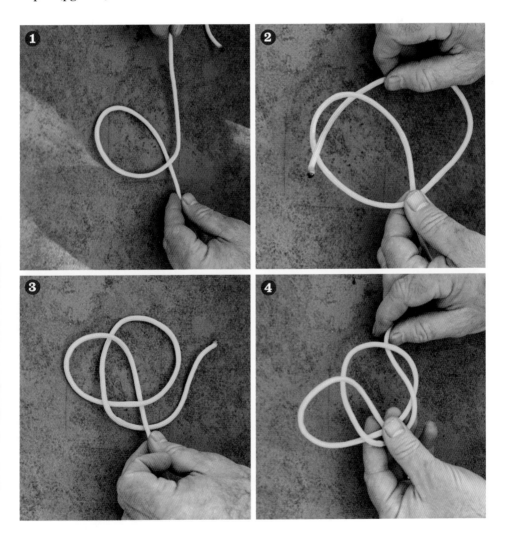

CAMP SECURITY

MAKING SURE EVERYTHING in your camp is safe and secure should be a top priority. As you'll soon discover, equipment costs a lot of money. And aside from the financial loss, having essential items stolen can force you to cut your trip short.

SAFE STORAGE

If you're camping in a tent (see site selection on pg. 78), the first thing you want to do is secure your items inside the tent with the zipper zipped all the way up. While "out of sight, out of mind" is usually effective for preventing theft, some people see a closed tent and realize there's a valuable item inside. Unfortunately, you can only do so much. For this reason, I keep small items of value, such as my compass, knife and ferro rod, on my person. At the very minimum, I know I have those three items and can still do many things should they become my only gear.

FIREARMS

Despite what some might picture, camp security does not involve a bunch of cowboys sitting around the fire at night with pistols on their hips and rifles hanging off their horses. Depending on where you camp, firearms may not be allowed. I am permitted to carry a handgun anywhere in Mississippi. I have a concealed carry permit and have extensive military training on how, when and why to use a firearm. But that's my experience, and yours is bound to be different. Firearms are not allowed in various parks and public lands throughout the country. Sometimes firearms can be carried, but it's still illegal to discharge one, no matter the reason. If camping on public land such as national and state parks, it's better not to have one on you at all. And if you are camping somewhere where firearms are legal, such as most national forests or wildlife areas, you should absolutely complete some gun safety training before carrying and using one. When you're not carrying it, store the firearm in your backpack or next to your sleeping gear.

Most wild animals scavenge for any quick and easy food source, and it doesn't get any quicker or easier than food left out by a human.

WILDLIFE

To ensure the safety of yourself and your campsite, you'll want to know what kinds of wildlife you might encounter in the area. For example, certain areas in Tennessee have black bears. If you're camping out there and carelessly leave food lying around, you could be putting yourself in danger. Animal attacks usually happen for two reasons: They perceive you as a threat to their young or you have food and they want it (or they believe you are the food). A bear will walk up to your camp at night; some can be skittish while others can be very aggressive. I know from living in Alaska that one of the most dangerous animals is a female moose—if she perceives you as a threat to her young, she will essentially stomp you into the ground and make sure you are dead.

To minimize contact with animals, secure your food and ensure it's out of reach. One measure you can take is to hang all food items in trees in a dry bag or animal-proof food storage container to keep them out of reach. You should also process, cook and eat your food in a location other than where you sleep. For instance, don't clean your fish outside your shelter then cook and eat it there as well. The smell will attract all sorts of critters from far and wide.

WHERE TO TAKE A BATHROOM BREAK

MANY NATIONAL AND state parks now require you to bring your number two out of the woods with you when you leave. Before you go, find out if this is a requirement so you can plan accordingly. For most sites, a latrine dug about 200 feet away from your camp will suffice, and this distance will also prevent flies and help with sanitation. And speaking of sanitary practices, remember to wash or sanitize your hands afterward.

Primitive camping often means foregoing conveniences such as outhouses.

TRENCH

The trench is an easy-to-make toilet alternative.

Step 1 At a spot 200 feet from camp, dig 6 to 8 inches deep and 12 inches wide. The length can be whatever you want. As you dig, pile your dirt up on the back edge of the trench.

Step 2 When you've finished your toilet break, cover your dirty business with the soil you dug out of the trench.

Step 3 Next time you have to use the trench, go next to where you buried the last one and keep going down the line.

HOLE

The hole is another easy alternative when you lack the luxury of a porta potty.

Step 1 Dig a deep hole about 200 feet from camp.

Step 2 Collect all the dirt from the hole in a pile. Every time you do your business, cover it with a bit of land and leaves just as you would with the trench.

Step 3 Continue until your trip is over (or until you fill the hole completely).

THINKING OUTSIDE THE BOX

WHEN IT COMES to camping, you always want to think about how to accomplish a specific task should you lack the tools designed to accomplish that task. What can you use to create the desired outcome from the limited inventory you have with you? You want to avoid being cornered into believing that everything can only be done a certain way. Thinking outside the box is nothing more than improvisation.

For instance, when it comes to fishing bait, you can simply use a piece of cotton; I've even caught largemouth bass with a bit of grass. And once you've caught and cleaned a fish, you can repurpose the entrails as bait to catch more fish; each fish you catch creates more bait to catch more fish.

First aid solutions also call for quick improvisation in the woods. You won't be carrying a full-fledged splint in your backpack—it would take up too much room. You can, however, find a sturdy stick and use it to improvise a splint. Or, if you injure your arm, you can use a handkerchief or a T-shirt to make a sling.

Thinking outside the box applies to everything from fishing, hunting, setting up your camp, first aid, and even cooking. Let's say you want biscuits for breakfast but didn't bring any flour. It's springtime, and you notice cattails in the stream or marshy area near you—you can collect the pollen from the cattails to use as flour. Once collected, the pollen should be sifted to remove any bugs or debris. The pollen is very fine and can be used as a flour substitute in many recipes. You can use cattail pollen to make pancakes, muffins, bread and other baked goods. It can also be used as a thickener in soups and stews.

Once you have collected all your pollen, you can take your stainless steel pot and use that as an oven by heaping coals on top of the pot to cook your biscuits (pg. 212).

These examples are meant to get you thinking. As stated before, there is no wrong way and no rules when it comes to primitive camping—it's simply about bringing what you need to survive and simultaneously making yourself comfortable. Once you get the hang of things, you'll be enjoying your time peacefully in the woods, not working yourself to death just to say you went camping.

In the following pages, I will break down primitive camping and bushcraft into the categories of gear, shelter, water, fire, food and cooking. As you explore the information and methods presented, go at your own pace. Find what works for you, and then gradually find ways to make it your own.

COLLECTING CATTAIL POLLEN

1. Find a patch of cattails (cattails are typically in bloom and produce pollen in the late spring or early summer).
2. Hold a bag or container under the cattail head and gently shake or tap the cattail to release the pollen. A dry, empty Gatorade bottle works great for this.
3. Repeat this process until you have collected enough pollen (each cattail should yield around 1 Tbsp of pollen).

In addition to being a flour alternative, cattail pollen is also a great source of protein.

CHAPTER 3

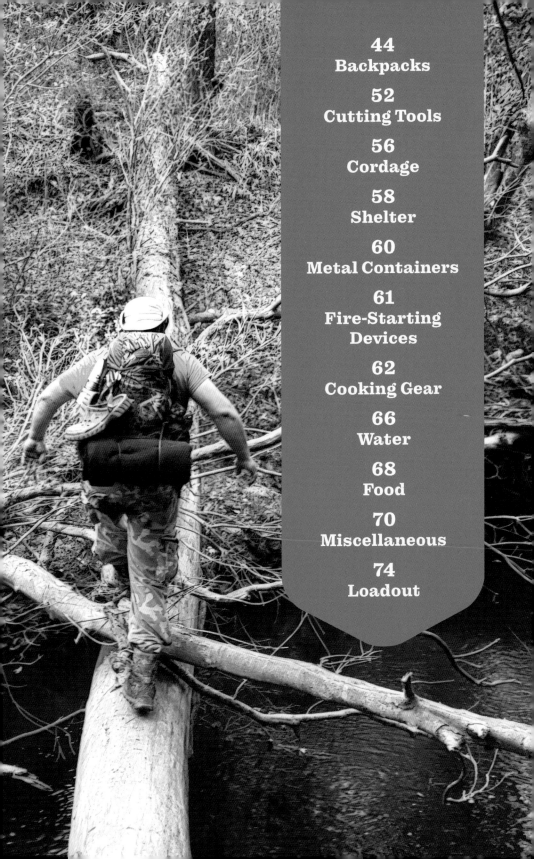

The more comfortable you are carrying and using your gear, the more you'll get to relax and enjoy the beautiful views of camping.

Welcome to the rabbit hole! According to *amateuradventurejournal.com*, camping gear in the United States accounts for $167 billion a year in sales. With a wide variety of equipment covering every aspect of camping, the prices range from "Wow, that's nothing!" to "Guess I'll get a second mortgage on the house...." But when it comes to camping gear, how much do you really need? It depends: How much can you carry?

Gear has an intended purpose for what you want to accomplish while camping. Sometimes you may bring items that turn out to be unnecessary or realize halfway through the journey that you need something you don't have. Frequent camping will build your experience level—to put it plainly, the more you go, the more you'll know. Each time you head into the great unknown, you will reflect on what you did the last time, what you needed and what you didn't need. No perfect gear loadout exists for primitive camping, survival or bushcraft. All the gear listed in this section is for your general reference to give you an idea of what you can and should be packing and what to leave behind.

BACKPACKS

BACKPACKS SERVE DIFFERENT
purposes and have infinite design
variations. For my first hiking
experience, I loaded a tactical-style
backpack with everything I thought I
would use—when I finished loading
it, the bag weighed nearly 40 pounds.
While that may seem correct given
my body weight calculations noted
earlier, tactical-style backpacks are
designed to hold less than 40 pounds
of gear. So, long story short, I was
pretty miserable! I had to stop every
30 minutes because, firstly, I was out
of shape, and secondly, the shoulder
straps cut off the circulation to my
arms. I was hunched over the entire
hike, and all the weight of the bag was
on my shoulders and knees.

After this trip, the first thing I did
was order a decent backpack for
hiking. What a difference! This new
pack had an internal frame and hip
straps that distribute the load to your
hips rather than your knees. I still
use it to this day. Are there better
backpacks on the market? Sure. And
if you can afford it, there is ultralight
backpacking gear that's heavy on the
wallet but light on the bulk. Personally,
I don't feel the need to replace what
isn't broken or spend top dollar on
something when half-price will do.
If you're new to hiking and primitive
camping, start with a cheaper internal
frame backpack with good hip straps
until you know what you really need,
then upgrade from there as you like.

When imagining your grand
adventures in primitive camping,
you may have had visions of hikers
carrying huge packs over long

It never hurts to double-check
that all the pockets on your
backpack are fully zipped.

distances as we have all seen on TV, like National Geographic explorers heading through the Amazon in search of ancient mysteries. Those packs carry everything—clothing, shelter, food, water, fire-starting tools—and the longer the trip, the heavier the backpack. But what you're carrying is irrelevant if you can't lift your pack. A conservative estimate for your own abilities is to set the max weight of your pack at 20 percent of your body weight. If I weigh 200 pounds, my pack should weigh 40 pounds or less. I realize many people weigh a lot less than I do, so I recommend trying to limit the weight of your pack to 30 pounds.

On a personal note, this is still a general guideline and not a rule—as an Air Force medic, my pack was 80 pounds, not including my body armor and weapon. But that doesn't mean I enjoyed toting it around on the trail.

The great woodsman and bushcraft instructor Mors Kochanski, author of *Bushcraft: Outdoor Skills and Wilderness Survival*, has a motto: "The more you know, the less you carry." The more you know about camping (pertaining to gear and living in the woods), the less you will need when you are in the woods. If you know how to build a stove or tripod for cooking, for example, you will not need to bring one. The same goes for all the other items and gear you carry into the woods. As stated before, when packing for a trip, you want to try to limit your load to multi-purpose items. If you have one item that can be used for more than one purpose, there is no need to load your backpack down with multiple items that do the same thing.

I prefer to take the approach of *Alone*, a survival competition show in which contestants are sent to the wilderness with nothing but the contents of their backpacks. They film themselves for the duration of the trip, procuring shelter, food and water in any way they choose. Contestants can only bring 10 items, including tools, shelter, clothing and cooking utensils. The last person to leave the wild is the winner. I figure if they

DOWNSIZING CAN BE AN UPGRADE

I recently upgraded to a 35-liter Pathfinder Scout backpack. How did I "upgrade" from 75 liters down to 35? Believe it or not, the Pathfinder Scout can hold just as much as the Amazon Basics pack with all the included straps on the outside. Now it's my go-to backpack. This pack has a soft internal frame built directly into it, hip straps and plenty of external pockets to keep the gear I need easily accessible. It helps me minimize my equipment by not getting overloaded with stuff I don't need.

can do it, so can I, so I try to limit my backpack to only 10 gear items. Depending on your situation, your mileage may vary, but as a general rule, try consolidating as much as possible. Start with only 10 items. Add a few more if you know you will need them or can't live without them.

When selecting backpacks and the gear you can pack, be realistic about what you're trying to accomplish. Are you going to establish a base camp and then travel to different overnight hunting sites? Or are you hiking 5 miles into the wilderness to set up camp and stay for several days? The former will require a lot more gear than the latter.

Backpacks are classed by volume. If you purchase a 75-liter bag, it should theoretically hold 75 liters of water (no, you are not going to fill your backpack with water). The measurement is obtained by measuring the volume of all the empty compartments, and some packs will include the external pockets. Still, generally speaking, if it is rated as a 75-liter, it should have 75 liters of volume to fill with your gear.

There are many materials used to make backpacks today. Canvas bags are incredibly durable and can endure years of abuse. They can be waxed or weather-sealed to keep them water-resistant, but compared to nylon packs, they are much heavier. Nylon is very lightweight and strong but will not withstand the abuse you can put a canvas bag through. With heavy use over the course of many trips, a nylon bag may start to fray and tear at the seams. Many newer backpacks come with a "raincoat" that is highly visible and fits over the bag to keep it

dry in wet weather and is usually built in, tucked away into a hidden pocket near the top or bottom of the bag. When selecting a backpack, ask two fundamental questions: How much do you really need to carry? How big does your backpack need to be? Too big of a pack encourages you to bring more than is required, and too small of pack forces you to decide between taking essential and non-essential gear. Once you've selected your bag and obtained some equipment, another question arises: How do you fit everything in there?

LOADING A BACKPACK

When gearing up for your trip, the heaviest or least used item is stowed on the bottom of the inside of your backpack. Let's say you are crossing a creek on a log—you don't want to move suddenly and have the bag's weight shift your balance causing you to fall into the water in the middle of winter. With the heavier items stowed lower, you maintain your center of gravity, which helps considerably with balance and is much more comfortable.

I always load my food, pots and pans first; they weigh the most and will nearly always be the last thing I pull out of the bag. From there, I load extra clothing, followed by a first aid kit and my hammock and tarp. On top of that, I will have my water filtration system. I stow my fire kit, cordage and metal water bottle in an easy-to-reach outside pocket. That way, I can quickly obtain a drink of water, start a fire or set up a ridge line for my tarp. I pack my bedroll and sleeping pad on the side or top (depending on which bag I'm using).

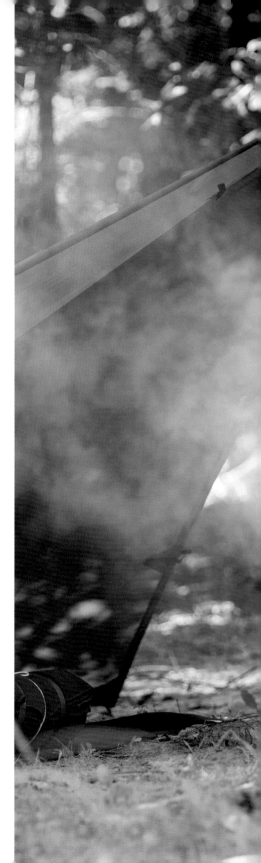

WHAT TO PACK

When I was an Air Force medic, we had a motto: "Always prepare for the worst and hope for the best." A great way to do that is to ensure you have a kit of what many in the industry refer to as your "EDC" or "everyday carry" with you at all times—but especially if you're will be camping out in the wild. Everything you carry into the woods should serve more than one purpose (there it is again!).

I have broken down primitive camping gear into five general areas. These areas are highly similar to what you would use for survival and bushcraft, as primitive camping is a blend of the two. Using these as the core building blocks of your equipment, you can build a complete primitive camping kit.

Cutting tools: knife, axe, saw
Cordage: rope, paracord, bank line
Shelter: tarp, tent, hammock, bedding
Metal containers: pot, water bottle
Fire-starting devices: Bic lighter, ferro rod, matches

Once you've selected your gear to meet these five areas, you can build upon and include other gear from the following categories:

QUICK TIP

Always pack one more pair of socks than you think you need.

A good hiking chair will give your body a much-needed break after setting up camp.

Cooking gear: stoves, utensils, containers
Water: gravity filter, purification tablets
Food: freeze-dried, dehydrated, ready to eat
Miscellaneous: gloves, flashlights, etc.

The five general areas can be added to or subtracted from depending on your skill set. I sometimes venture out with less than the five areas listed, and you may require more. It all depends on your comfort level and experience with or without these items.

Cutting tools such as a knife, axe and saw are used extensively around camp, from cleaning food and building shelter to starting and maintaining your fire. Your knife will be used around camp more than any other tool, but it is also handy to have access to an axe or saw if you need to cut larger logs or trees.

Cordage is used to tie down your tarps, tents and hammocks and build any other convenience you can dream up in the woods. String or rope will allow you to fish (if you don't carry a roll of fishing line), hang pots and lash up a tripod for cooking.

When it comes to shelter, tarps are my number-one choice. You cannot beat the versatility of a lightweight, good-quality tarp. It can collect your water, protect you from the rain and wind and even be used around a tripod to make a smoker for your food (be careful not to burn holes in it). Tarps can be used to create numerous shelter variations, making them useful in multiple climates.

Metal containers are perfect for collecting and boiling water, cooking and sometimes digging a hole.

Having a reliable way to start a fire in the woods is paramount! You must practice your fire-starting methods before venturing out into the wilderness. You also want to know and follow the fire rules for your camping area. Let's break down each of these five generalized gear areas even further.

A shemagh can be used as headwear, a water filter and a way to carry wood.

You may want to try out various tools before deciding what makes the cut for future trips.

CUTTING TOOLS

THE SINGLE MOST important item you will carry with you into the woods is a knife. I covered knife selection in great detail in the introduction (pg. 18), so we will discuss axes and saws here. A good axe or saw can also be extremely useful in the woods, especially for dealing with larger trees and logs. There are so many variations of axes, each with a particular design for specific reasons. An axe I use may not work for you. I heard once that an axe is like a pair of shoes: I may think it's awesome, but you may hate it. It may be comfortable for me to swing but give you blisters. I have used a "utility" axe for years, meaning it serves more than one purpose: It can cut trees, split firewood and carve if needed. The felling axe is an example of what you will typically find when shopping for primitive camping gear. This axe is designed for chopping trees and cutting branches. Thanks to its heavy head and long handle, it can be swung very powerfully. The handle of this axe is usually made from hickory but there are also synthetic handles so you don't break them when splitting logs. As with any axe, the only drawback is the weight it will add to your pack. But you have to ask yourself: Will the benefit of having an axe outweigh the burden of the extra weight?

The hatchet is a multipurpose tool and is the type of axe typically associated with camping. Hatchets are small compared to other axes, and their benefits range from pounding stakes into the ground to cutting thinner trees to splitting firewood. Some individuals pack a hatchet rather

The appeal of a multitool is in the name—this item can accomplish several tasks around your campsite.

than a knife and use it for all their carving and cleaning wild game. It may look funny to cut up a fish with an axe, but it works. I personally use a knife for this task and leave the axes for chopping and carving.

Estwing makes a Long Handle Camper's Axe that is somewhere between a felling axe and a hatchet. It's constructed as one piece of steel and has a shorter handle than a felling axe at 26 inches long. I've been using this axe for more than 10 years—it's light enough to carry on my backpack and just the right size for hatchet work (but also long enough to cut down large trees). The Camper's Axe can usually be picked up at a local home improvement store and is not as expensive as some of the other name-brand axes on the market. Axes vary widely in price depending on style, brand and function.

Doing a little research ahead of time will help you make the best purchase for your personal preferences. As with any tool you take camping, you want to select an axe that is good for multiple tasks, such as chopping down a tree, splitting logs and carving. Another thing you want to consider is how to keep your axe sharp while camping. This may not be an issue if you're only going to be camping for a few days, but with heavy use, your axe will become dull—and a dull tool is a dangerous tool. Consider using a puck to keep your axe sharp. A puck is a round sharpening stone that resembles a hockey puck and can sharpen an axe, hatchet or knife. If you don't carry a puck, you can also use the file on your multi-tool, a smooth stone from a creek or river or even the bottom of a porcelain coffee cup.

A saw is another versatile item to carry with you. I will often only bring a knife and folding saw as my cutting tools. There are so many variations that it can be difficult to determine which type is needed, but it all comes down to what you're planning to use it for. Do you intend to cut thick logs? Or do you plan on cutting smaller items around camp to make utensils and cooking appliances? There are bucksaws, bow saws, folding saws, blades for cutting green wood and deadwood—the options are endless. My go-to is a relatively small folding saw called the Bahco Laplander. This saw folds up nicely and fits perfectly into a side pocket on my pack. It cuts smaller diameter logs (up to 6 inches) with minimal effort and it allows me to make pot cranes and notches for cooking with green wood. I have even used a blade from a bow saw before and made the actual handle with materials found in the woods. I have also made my own bucksaw, but it is much more convenient to bring a folding saw.

Buck saws are designed to cut larger logs that you then split with your axe to the desired size for firewood. This is helpful when you're in the woods for extended periods because you can process large quantities of wood.

The brand Silky has more extensive versions of the folding saw designed to cut very large logs (12 inches in diameter or larger). Still, I personally prefer the Laplander. A good quality saw can also be used as a striker for your ferro rod to start a fire if needed. I used a cheap bow saw from a local home improvement store for many years. This saw is great because it allows me to cut more extensive material, but the downside is it's very bulky and doesn't fit onto my backpack very well. There are newer versions of the bow saw on the market today that fold up and are very lightweight and packable. My approach with equipment is to get more bang for your buck, which is why I chose to switch to a folding saw that is compact and multi-use.

CORDAGE

CORDAGE IS ANOTHER name for strings or ropes. This rope will be used to make other tools or conveniences around your camp. It's best to carry some variation of cordage—I'm not trying to discourage you from making natural cordage, but while primitive camping, you do not want to spend all your time making rope when you could be enjoying your time outdoors. Making primitive rope is relatively easy but very time-consuming. String made from yucca or the inner bark of a willow tree can be very robust. Certain young roots from pine trees and various vines can be used as cordage in a pinch.

I carry 100 feet of paracord and a roll of #36 or #48 bank line, a nylon cord similar to tennis netting, in my pack. Paracord is handy because it contains seven strands of nylon inside a braided nylon sheath of 32 interwoven strands—which means if you cut a 5-foot section and remove the seven strands and tie them together, you would have 35 feet of fishing line and can use the 5-foot casing for other things. This sheath or case is impressive when used in conjunction with an arbor or jam knot (pg. 31) when making your own handle for a buck saw. When paired with this material, the jam knot holds exceptionally tight.

For nearly the same price as 100 feet of paracord, you can get 125 yards of bank line. The number designation is the diameter of the line (#36 bank line, for example, is perfect for outdoor tasks), so a smaller number equals thinner string with equivalent length.

I use bank line for catfishing, bow drills and guylines for tarps and tents. Tarred and twisted nylon bank line has a 340-pound breaking strength. Growing up, the only name I knew this string by was "trotline." Trotlining is a method of fishing where you run a line across the water while setting stages

or using a Prusik knot (pg. 30) with hooks to catch catfish. In southern Mississippi and Louisiana, you can string out five trotlines with five or more hooks on them and fill your boat with fresh catfish in no time.

You will get more bang for your buck with a roll of tarred and twisted bank line than with paracord. Bank line has three strands twisted together that can be untwisted and used for thread to sew your torn clothing or fishing string. Broken down even further, you can use bank line as an excellent tinder to get a good fire burning.

Be sure your setup prevents smoke from reaching your shelter.

SHELTER

WHILE THERE IS an entire chapter on what shelter is and how to set it up (pg. 76), it's crucial to note the importance of carrying some items for coverage or protection from the elements. "Shelter" is all about making a "micro-climate," and the first stage of shelter is the clothing you have on. For example, a military poncho serves multiple purposes. You can use it to keep dry during the rain, set it up as a practical shelter or use it as a rain catch for collecting drinking water. Whenever I go camping, I take a 9-by-9 tarp, which has served me well for years. But even contractor-grade garbage bags can be used as a rain poncho, a rain catch, an emergency shelter and even a mattress. Hammocks combined with a tarp for coverage make an excellent shelter. I can use a hammock for a shelter year-round in south Mississippi. In other geographic locations, you may want to limit hammock use to late spring, summer and early fall. I use a hammock with a built-in bug screen because nothing is worse than the vampire-esque mosquitoes in the

QUICK TIP

Extra cordage will often come in handy when setting shelter.

back pain or other injuries. I was once asked to review a 3-pound portable cot that folds up and fits on a backpack—that cot changed my thoughts on sleeping in a tent. It was comfortable, and I didn't wake up with back pain from sleeping on the hard ground. Depending on where you camp and the size of your tent, this added luxury may be an option. Tents do tend to weigh more than hammocks, however, making a hammock more appealing to many people. One of the biggest downfalls to a tent is the condensation buildup. When you exhale inside a zipped tent, the warm moisture meets the cool air around the tent and condenses on the walls. Living in a tent in these conditions for an extended period leads to mold growth. Still, you will not always be camping in a place conducive to hanging a hammock; if you do use a tent, you will need some type of mattress pad or ground cloth to lay on the ground. Some people like sleeping on the ground without one, but the same concept of convection cooling still applies. The ground will nearly always be cooler than your body temperature, and the earth will suck the warmth out of your body. For this reason, any variation of ground barrier is recommended. Mattress pads come in several varieties, from self-inflating, foot pump and inflatable to foam pads.

swamps of south Mississippi!

An underquilt prevents warmth from escaping via convective cooling. When your body temperature exceeds the air temperature, convective cooling sucks up all your body heat. This phenomenon is horrible during winter, late fall and early spring without an underquilt or sleeping pad. Using a hammock underquilt, I have slept very comfortably in below-freezing temperatures, high winds and rain.

A tent provides excellent shelter outdoors. But some people do not like sleeping on the ground due to

METAL CONTAINERS

A METAL CONTAINER, such as a nesting canteen or a pot, is invaluable on a trek into the wilderness. One of the biggest trends in the outdoor world today is the metal water bottle. They are everywhere, from the dollar store to Bass Pro Shops. Do not carry a double-insulated water bottle, as it will explode if used to boil water. Always use a single-wall metal container. Boiling your water (pg. 107) is one of the most critical aspects of primitive camping, survival and bushcraft. The vast majority of the time, you will collect, boil and drink water you have fetched from a stream, river or lake. Boiling your water will ensure that all the biological contaminants (but unfortunately not the chemical pollutants) have been neutralized and rendered safe to drink.

A metal container will also allow you to make charred material for fire-starting and carry water and store food or other items. I use a relatively small 27-ounce stainless steel pot with a lid when I venture into the woods. It's lightweight and robust, and I have used it for countless tasks including digging fire pits, Dakota fire holes (pg. 244) and latrines and, of course, cooking dinner. But ultimately, having a metal container is essential for boiling your water and making it safe to drink. If you have a metal container, no matter how nasty the water source is, you will always be able to make drinkable water.

QUICK TIP

A pot gripper is a helpful tool that allows you to safely grab and lift a hot metal container.

No one wants to carry and clean multiple metal containers—find one that works for many purposes.

A ferro rod will quickly become one of your most used items around camp.

FIRE-STARTING DEVICES

FIRE CAN BE COMPLEX and tricky, which is why it's best to carry multiple ways to start a fire. A Bic lighter is the easiest and most cost-effective fire-starting device in modern times and is one of the items you should have more than one of. Buy them in bulk and make a habit of carrying one in your camping kit, your pocket, your first aid kit, your backpack and your fire kit (pg. 162). That way, you will always have a backup. A ferrocerium rod or "ferro rod" is also essential. With enough practice, a 6-by-½-inch ferro rod is good for thousands of strikes and, realistically, thousands of fires. A magnification lens is also an excellent addition to any kit. Starting a fire with a magnification lens only requires a sunny day and minimal effort, depending on your geographic location and the time of year. For more on fire kits and step-by-step instructions for starting a fire with each of these items, see the Fire section (pg. 138).

Once you have selected your core items, you can choose broader pieces of gear for your camping experience. As stated, you can expand beyond the five generalized gear categories to include cooking gear, water, food and miscellaneous items.

A foldable hiking stove is one of the most convenient cooking items you can carry.

COOKING GEAR

COOKING GEAR CAN include grills, stoves, solar ovens and any other device or apparatus used to cook or warm your food and kill any harmful biological pathogens (pg. 60). Stoves come in all shapes and sizes, from fold-up and compact to large wood-burning stoves that double as heaters for a tent. For the primitive camper, depending on the environment in which you camp, the folding wood-burning stove is perfect. This little bundle of joy is called a bio stove or biomass stove. They can use essentially anything that will burn as fuel—leaves, sticks, twigs and paper, to name a few. Depending on your environment, you should always be able to find something to burn, even in desert areas. But be careful when burning vines and certain cacti, as the smoke can cause chemical burns, leading to blindness, respiratory burns and even death. For instance, if you burn poison ivy or sumac, the oils from the plant are released in the smoke and an allergic reaction can occur when the smoke comes in contact with your eyes or you inhale it.

The folding wood-burning stove has been a staple item in my backpack for many years. If I am not open-fire roasting, I am using the wood-burning stove. It's effortless to transport, use and maintain the proper cooking temperature. If you want to warm some water for coffee, throw in some leaves and you are on your way. These stoves come in stainless steel (which I use) and titanium (which is extremely lightweight), and both are perfect for hikers and campers. There is another type of wood-burning stove,

the LHOKA T Castle, that you have to assemble in the shape of a castle. These little gems come in stainless steel or titanium as well. The titanium variant weighs 6 to 8 ounces, while the stainless version weighs slightly less than a pound. Once assembled, this stove has a hole in the front to which you add your biomaterial and air holes all around the sides. It has an open top where you rest the pot for cooking and is easy to use and operate.

Grills have made similar advancements in recent years. Today, grills are made from stainless steel and titanium and are very compact and portable compared to those of the past. I bought mine at a local department store for only $4, and it has served me countless times in the woods. It's easy to pack and even easier to use. Just rake some coals from your fire to the side, throw the grill on top and you're ready to cook. You can adjust the cooking temperature by adding twigs and sticks as needed (but it's best to cook over hot coals rather than open flames).

The Bedroll Cooker is another excellent option; it has a waxed canvas sleeve/pouch to keep all your gear from getting covered in soot and is entirely adjustable and maneuverable. It also has three small poles that hook together and can be driven into the ground. You then hang your small grill or bottle hook on the poles and they stay in place by friction caused by gravity. This option is reminiscent of how soldiers cooked food on an open fire during the Civil War with a similar but much larger (and heavier) wrought iron system.

Once you are above the timberline

Take your cooking to the next level: a Bedroll Cooker (top); a propane stove (bottom left); a pot used as an oven (top right); a cast iron pot (bottom right).

on a mountain range, biofuel can be scarce, so propane stoves are best. These ultra-lightweight titanium stoves are extraordinarily compact. They work great for a single person, but there are better options for those camping in groups. One of the main downfalls of propane stoves is the propane fuel itself. You have to carry additional weight, the amount of fuel is finite and your trip can last longer than your fuel source. But one of the best benefits of the propane stove is that you can use one during an open fire ban. Check with your local state authorities to see which option is allowed before you head out.

Solar ovens are neat little devices.

> **QUICK TIP**
> Aluminum foil is a lightweight means of cooking food over fire.

They look like coffee thermoses and can boil water and cook food—but if it's a cloudy day, you will not be satisfied with the results. Some brands claim to work even when the sky is overcast, but a good rule of thumb is if you can't start a fire with a magnification lens on a given day, chances are you can't use a solar oven to cook food either.

Bedroll Cookers uses pegs for elevated cooking over a fire.

WATER

BEFORE WE DO a deep dive into water (pg. 100), let's explore the gear you can use to obtain clean drinking water. There are hundreds of ways to collect, filter and purify your water, but it's important to note: Filtering and purifying are not the same process! Filtering removes debris and contaminants, whereas purifying makes your water biologically safe to consume. The easiest way to purify your water and make it drinkable is to boil it.

The simplest way to "filter" your water is with an ordinary handkerchief or shemagh (a tactical military scarf). Now, you can't just say "Cheers!" and drink your fill of this water; it still has to be boiled. A millbank bag can also filter out all the dirt and grime. Resembling a Christmas stocking made from a heavy canvas material, these bags soak in the water source for several minutes so the fibers expand. Then, you fill it roughly three-quarters full and hang it on a tree branch with a metal container underneath it. The water drips out free of silt, dirt and debris (even the extra protein, like tadpoles). Once your cup is full, it's ready to boil.

Commercial water filters are a straightforward, cost-effective way to make safe drinking water. These ubiquitous products can filter down to .001 microns, and a virus cell ranges from .005 to .3 microns in size. A ceramic water filtration device can potentially filter out viruses in drinking water—the key word being "potentially" because, with any manufactured item, there is always room for error.

Many hikers and campers (myself included) use straw or squeeze bag systems to obtain clean water when trekking. With these systems, it's important to use a pre-filter like a millbank bag or, at the very minimum, a handkerchief to get all the debris out of your water before using your filter. If not, it will clog. I was once on a 10-day trip when my straw and squeeze bag filter clogged up. Even though the water appeared crystal clear and clean, because I did not pre-filter it, I had to make a tripod water filter to filter the water (pg. 122).

One of my favorite ways to filter water is with a gravity-fed system. The one I use has a 6-liter reservoir bag that is filled with water from the source. Then, you let the water run down a hose and through a ceramic filter cartridge into the drinking container. This system is easy to use and filters a large quantity of water while you are busy doing other things around camp. The straw variety is one of the more popular types of personal water filters. They are straightforward to use, filter large quantities of water before clogging and are disposable and cheap to replace.

No matter the type of filtration system you choose, it's wise to also bring some variation of a commercial water filter on your trip. Not only are they easy to find when shopping for gear, they're also very convenient and effective.

QUICK TIP

A collapsible water container will save space, but it may not have the durability of other vessels.

6L
GRAVITY-FED
WATER SYSTEM

Membrane Solutions

For more on the benefits of gravity-fed water systems, see pg. 132.

Planning which items you'll eat on each day will ensure you have enough food for your trip.

FOOD

FOOD EQUALS CALORIES, and calories equal energy. When camping, you expend tons of calories that you otherwise would not in your daily life. When heading outdoors, plan how many days you will be gone and how much food you'll need. Do you plan to fish or hunt for your food? Or do you plan on bringing your own food? I carry a limited quantity of food and supplement it with hunting and fishing (see Optional Load, pg. 72). Outdoor stores have many varieties of freeze-dried foods available, but they tend to be high in salt. Because of this, I make my camp food by using a dehydrator, which is a very cost-effective and useful tool.

Before we go over a full grocery list of food items (pg. 182), you'll want to start thinking about what you will bring versus how much it weighs.

A few options to consider are (heaviest to lightest):

Canned meats
Summer sausage (doesn't require refrigeration)
Dried beans
Instant or regular rice
JAW (Just Add Water) meals
Prepackaged, ready-to-eat meals
Packet mashed potatoes
Freeze-dried foods

MISCELLANEOUS

THIS CATEGORY IS for "all the other stuff" you may want on hand while camping. At the minimum, a good flashlight is one fairly essential item: You can camp without one (which I've done unintentionally), but life is much simpler if you bring it along. I personally get a lot of use out of a cheap headlamp made by Energizer— the only drawback is it uses batteries. Three triple-A batteries don't weigh much, but I can't tell you how many

times I forgot to pack replacements and had to go without a light source partway through my trip. For that reason, a small, rechargeable LED handheld flashlight is an excellent addition to any camping kit as it allows you to see greater distances than a headlamp and can be fully charged before you head out.

Another miscellaneous item I carry is a very lightweight solar lantern. It easily fits into my kit and it can light

Inset top to bottom: first aid kid bag; headlamp; solar lantern (in use at left).

hands from blisters and splinters when splitting wood and keep you from getting burned when working with fire. For instance, I once dispatched an armadillo in my camp, skinned it and cooked it. Armadillos have the potential to carry leprosy, and by using gloves, I had a protective barrier from any possible infection. Gloves are also handy when clearing out a location for your shelter as you may need to pull thorny vines down.

A multi-tool is another item that can prove invaluable. This piece of gear can be classified as a cutting tool, but one from a reputable brand can help with many tasks. I have used the pliers from a multi-tool when cooking, setting squirrel traps, tightening loose nuts and bolts and for countless other tasks. The multi-tool's saw is great for making cooking utensils, notches on a pot crane and other helpful tools.

As for additional bedding, there is no substitute for a wool blanket. A genuine 100 percent wool blanket will keep you warm on cold and wet nights. A sleeping bag made from quality natural feather down or synthetic material can also be useful, but the climate you're camping in should always determine the type of bag you select. A natural down bag, for example, is extremely difficult to dry once it gets wet.

Synthetic material is easier to dry if it becomes damp, but it doesn't keep you as warm as natural feather down. There are, however, incredibly lightweight down-stuffed blankets that are 100 percent waterproof on the market. I have been using one for a few years in conjunction with my wool blanket and have stayed very warm in

up the entire camp for over 20 hours without using any fuel or mantles (nylon socks used to create light in the lantern), requiring just a few hours in the sun to recharge. Two solar lanterns provide enough light for your entire camp, extending the battery life of your headlamp. Solar lanterns are also excellent additions to an emergency kit around your home in the event of power failure from natural disasters such as tornadoes, hurricanes and earthquakes.

Leather gloves are another good item to have with you. They protect your a hammock when the temperature was in the low-to-mid 30s.

If you're looking for extra comfort while camping, lightweight hiking or camping chairs can help. Many modern chairs fold up very small and can easily fit on your backpack. Sitting on stumps and logs is fine, but after a few days, your back will begin to ache from the lack of support—which will make carrying your backpack out of the woods quite uncomfortable.

As mentioned in the introduction (pg. 12), it's always wise to carry even a basic first aid kit whenever possible. This will allow you to take care of yourself in the event of minor injuries and also assist anyone you may encounter who needs help. A basic first aid kit should have you covered from blisters to cuts and even some significant injuries.

On pg. 74 you'll find everything I would take on a 10-day trip in the wilderness of south Mississippi.

I have used this exact gear load for years and enjoyed all my trips into the woods. At approximately 29 pounds, depending on the axe, this loadout is

Factors such as weather may cause you to modify your gear load, opting for a tent rather than a hammock, for example.

LuminAID solar lanterns are waterproof and feature adjustable brightness.

not too bulky, is easy to manage and allows me to stay comfortable for an extended period. A lot of the weight is due to food; the more food, the more bulk and weight.

OPTIONAL LOAD

Instead of a hammock, I will sometimes bring a small two-person tent. The tent also straps to the outside of the backpack.

If you choose to fish rather than to carry a lot of food, a small fishing kit is straightforward to assemble and won't add too much weight. I have several

sizes of fish hooks, a packet of split shot weights and 100 yards of fishing string (which has multiple uses). Including a few rubber worms or grubs can improve the chances of catching a largemouth bass or two, spinning baits such as a beetle spin significantly enhance the opportunity to catch pike and bass and a few small bobbers or corks can help you reel in panfish such as bluegill. Live bait is plentiful in the woods; lizards, worms, grubs, crickets and grasshoppers are almost always found near water.

Once again, this is not the end-all-be-all guide to camping gear but rather a generalized overview to get you thinking about what you really need and what you can go without. With the countless items out there today, choosing camping gear really comes down to your desired level of comfort and budget. Don't feel like you need to collect everything all at once—gear is something better acquired over a period of time. As long as you stick to the five general areas of camping gear, you can comfortably travel long distances and enjoy your time in the woods.

LOADOUT

Here's an example of all the gear you might pack for a trip.

BACKPACK
1. 35-liter Pathfinder Scout pack

TOP POCKET
2. Handkerchief (pre-washed if colored)
3. Topographical map of the area
4. Compass (Suunto M-3)
5. Straw water filter
6. Extra knife (Morakniv Companion HeavyDuty)
7. Headlight or headlamp
8. Bic lighter (bright color)
9. Folding saw (Bahco Laplander)

BACK BOTTOM POCKET
10. Fire kit
11. Paracord and bank line
12. Roll of 26-gauge floral wire (perfect for squirrel traps and hanging fish to smoke)

OUTSIDE SIDE POCKET
13. Metal water bottle (24-oz aluminum single-wall)

INSIDE THE BACKPACK (FROM BOTTOM TO TOP)
14. Change of clothing (or heavier jacket)

15. Small fishing kit
16. First aid kit
17. Hammock
18. Tarp
19. Water filtration bag (gravity water filter)
20. Leather gloves
21. Stainless steel pot (heavy and bulky, food items will fit inside of pot)
22. Stainless steel bio stove (folds up nice and neat and fits inside of pot)
23. Food (1 pound dried beans, 1 pound rice, freeze-dried meals, drink packets)

STRAPPED TO THE OUTSIDE OF THE BACKPACK
24. Wool blanket (with flat sheet rolled up inside)
25. Axe (if I chose to bring one)
26. Hiking chair
27. Solar lantern
28. Collapsible fishing rod and reel

STRAPPED TO THE BOTTOM OF THE BACKPACK
29. Inflatable sleeping mat (if needed)

W hat do you think of when you think of shelter? The first thing that probably comes to mind is your house. Our homes are shelters that provide shade from the sun on hot days and protection from the rain and snow on cold, wet ones. Most homes have air conditioning, heating, cooking appliances and plumbing, all of which make life easier and more comfortable. But it wasn't very long ago that we didn't have running water in our houses. There was no such thing as air conditioning and the heat came from a big wood-burning stove that cooked our food and warmed the house simultaneously.

Your shelter during a camping trip will do the same thing on a much smaller scale and in a way that resembles how homes used to be. A tent, hammock or tarp will protect you from the elements, but first, you have to know what to look for in a campsite. There are many different options out there, from developed camping sites designed for RVs and travel trailers, equipped with water and electricity, to primitive camping areas with fire rings already in place. Some public lands will only allow you to camp in designated areas or at preexisting structures, and the majority already have established locations for you to pitch a tent. But let's imagine that we walked 5 or 6 miles into the woods and we're looking for a suitable and safe place to build our shelter, set up our tent or hang our hat—well, hammock.

Other aspects of site selection to consider are proximity to drinking water and availability of firewood. A water source should be close to your

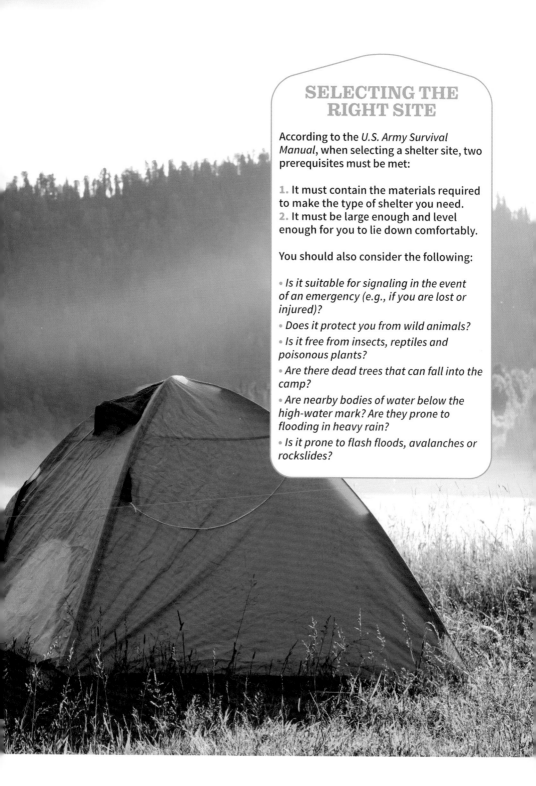

SELECTING THE RIGHT SITE

According to the *U.S. Army Survival Manual*, when selecting a shelter site, two prerequisites must be met:

1. It must contain the materials required to make the type of shelter you need.
2. It must be large enough and level enough for you to lie down comfortably.

You should also consider the following:

- *Is it suitable for signaling in the event of an emergency (e.g., if you are lost or injured)?*
- *Does it protect you from wild animals?*
- *Is it free from insects, reptiles and poisonous plants?*
- *Are there dead trees that can fall into the camp?*
- *Are nearby bodies of water below the high-water mark? Are they prone to flooding in heavy rain?*
- *Is it prone to flash floods, avalanches or rockslides?*

campsite—you want to avoid walking a mile to collect drinking water and then walking another mile back to boil it. Try to avoid camping next to stagnant water. The last thing you want to drink from is a stagnant pool or pond with a dead animal or a bunch of otters, nutrias or beavers swimming around, unless that's the only water source available (for filtering stagnant water, see pg. 112).

Your proximity to water will contribute to increased encounters with animals and those notorious little vampires known as mosquitoes. However, being closer to water will help with another aspect of primitive camping not covered in this chapter: procuring food. When camping close to water, you can easily fish, set snares, catch frogs and snakes. If it walks, hops, slithers or flies, it can be eaten. There are exceptions to this on each continent; certain critters are poisonous, so be careful and be sure you know your target food source.

Dragging firewood back to camp can also be very tiring, and you don't want to expend all your calories on a single task. Select a site with plenty of downed trees and limbs. You don't want to burn completely rotten wood, though; it doesn't produce much heat because it's less dense than solid firewood. I spend a lot of time collecting wood after I set up my camp so that I always have enough wood ready to burn before bed.

One crucial and often overlooked aspect of site selection is the presence of dead-standing trees called widowmakers, which could fall into camp when the wind picks up and cause serious injury or death. Most people look around the campsite to ensure they don't have one of these nearby, but they forget about the ones that are 80 or 90 feet away that still might be tall enough to crash into the campsite. You can use a dead tree to your advantage, however: Push it over, knock it down or cut it down and add it to your firewood collection. Just be sure to do so as safely as possible.

Mosquitoes and biting insects can be a considerable nuisance, and the best way to help control them is with a very smoky fire. Burning certain weeds and trees such as dogfennel, which grows in North America, can deter insects. You can rub this weed onto your skin and clothing or lay it into the coals to give off smoke that works exceptionally well for keeping these pests at bay. Burning pine or other resinous trees can help control various insects as well, and the green leaves from these resinous trees can also be burned to fend off mosquitoes in particular.

When selecting your shelter site, you also want to make sure you're not in an area where flash floods can occur. When you choose a site near water, you want to be able to see a high-water mark on the trees. This indicates how much the water level has risen from the previous flooding. The water leaves a dirt ring around the tree and is usually a good indicator that you are in a flood area.

In mountainous regions, avoid building your shelter near places prone to avalanches in the winter or rockslides in other seasons. These areas can provide significant natural shelter—a shelter created from rocks significantly increases the reflectivity of heat, and the stones themselves absorb heat, creating a warmer environment

MUD RING →

In this photo, the high-water mark is the middle ring over the white line on the tree.

in colder climates. But caution should always be used when choosing a site like this.

Shelter can also be all-natural, with common examples being rock formations, caves and hollow trees. If your surroundings don't provide a safe, convenient natural shelter, making one out of natural (or select man-made) materials can provide some protection from the elements (pg. 98).

Cover from the elements should be a priority in a survival situation. Imagine you are canoeing down a river alone when you suddenly capsize and all your gear floats away, leaving you with no supplies and no way to call for help. In that scenario, you would want to start looking for shelter as soon as possible. But, as primitive campers, we usually have our protection with us (or on us)

MIND THE WATER MARK

Here's a cautionary tale about paying attention to that high-water mark. Years ago, I was camping on the Pearl River in southern Mississippi. It wasn't raining when I arrived and there was no rain in the forecast for the week. I found a nice little area near the river perfect for fishing, plus there was plenty of firewood lying around. One morning, I woke up to water coming inside the tent. It had rained north of me that night, and all the water flowed south and caused the river to rise. Within an hour, my entire campsite was under 2 feet of water.

and can adapt at a moment's notice. So, we must look at all aspects of shelter to understand what it truly is.

YOUR CLOTHING IS your first layer of shelter. Depending on your environment, your clothing protects you from insects, sun, wind and rain. Rather than getting into the weeds of "seasonal clothing," at minimum, you should dress for the occasion or environment. Have you ever noticed that in photos from the 1800s, everyone is wearing long pants and either a long-sleeved shirt or jacket, even in the summer? Their clothing was made from linen, cotton or wool and it kept them cooler by absorbing their sweat. It also protected them from the sun and insects during the warmer months. In the winter, wool clothing kept them warm.

I recommend wearing long pants and a lightweight long-sleeved shirt whenever you venture into the woods. One of the main reasons is protection from insects. I don't know about you, but mosquitoes love me just as much as Jesus does!

Relatively loose-fitting long-sleeved clothing allows you to stay cool in hotter environments and warm in cooler climates. In hot environments, removing your clothing will cause you to lose sweat and require more sweat to cool you off, which could contribute to dehydration. So, when it comes to camping, leave your clothes on—it's OK to be stinky! Just hit the creek, river or lake to wash up; you can even collect some water in your metal pot and warm it up to have hot water for a quick rag bath.

You also want to dress in layers. Layering your clothing allows you to maintain your body temperature.

PORTABLE, MULTIPURPOSE ITEM

A shemagh is a multiuse item that can not only filter your water and protect your head from the sun and elements but can also be used to carry firewood. Using the shemagh to carry or bundle firewood can significantly speed up the task, especially for smaller material. A standard shemagh is usually made from cotton and measures 44 by 44 inches. It's essentially a giant handkerchief.

If it gets too hot, take a layer off; if it gets too cold, put it back on. Hunters, hikers and campers use this method all the time. For a good base layer, use thermal underwear, then a long-sleeved shirt, then an outer layer such as a jacket or overalls. This can keep you warm on the coldest days, regulate your microclimate and prevent hypothermia.

The material your clothing is made from can also significantly impact your comfort in the wilderness. All-natural, synthetic, blended and moisture-wicking are among the many materials available, and your environment should inform your clothing type. For example, cotton is incredible in warm weather. One characteristic of cotton is that it soaks up moisture—it can even be used to wick and filter dirty water (pg. 110). However, some survival experts claim that wet cotton T-shirts do not protect against sunburn. While living in Alaska for four years, I discovered firsthand that once cotton gets wet, it loses all of its insulative properties. Damp cotton clothing must be dried out in colder environments because, if left on in the cold, it can cause hypothermia, which can be fatal. There's an old saying in the survival community: "Cotton kills."

Unlike cotton, wool is excellent in both warm and cold climates. Wool is highly breathable and wicks moisture away from your body, keeping you dry. It's also naturally anti-bacterial, which helps keep body odor at bay. Wool keeps you warm even when wet as it retains its insulative properties when completely soaked, making wool socks a must for cold, damp camping trips. Plus, wool is wrinkle-resistant,

QUICK TIP
A sun hat or other headwear is crucial for protecting your head from the sun's rays.

so you can always look your best, even while camping. The only downside of wool is that it's heavy, especially when wet. Fortunately, wool clothing can be wrung out and put back on. The same goes for wool blankets—a good 80- to 100-percent wool blanket will keep you warm even when soaking wet. Wool gives the impression of being itchy and uncomfortable, but modern advancements have made it just as comfortable as cotton. Be wary: Some clothing labeled "wool" is actually polyester fleece. Some materials are used to imitate wool, but they do not insulate as well.

Some synthetic clothing materials on the market today are waterproof or water-resistant. Most of these are made from petroleum-based polymers which are then heated, melted, made into very fine fiber and woven into thread. These synthetics are usually blended with cotton or other natural fibers to create clothing for sports and outdoor activities. Polyester is among the most common of these materials, and nylon is another with plenty of uses beyond clothing, including tarps and hammocks. I try to stick to merino wool or wool and cotton blends, which offer both comfort and durability. If a spark from your ferro rod bounces off the log onto your arm, you don't want it to melt a hole in your sleeve. If you are wearing wool, you'll be protected since it's naturally fire-retardant.

TENTS

WHEN MOST PEOPLE visualize camping, the first thing that comes to mind is usually a tent next to a fire. Tents are just like all other gear on the market today—they vary depending on preference. Newer tents are incredibly lightweight and versatile, but you still want to choose the best option for your needs. Large "family" tents can be extremely heavy and are not very fun to carry on a primitive camping trip deep into the woods, but they are nice and roomy. A small two-person tent gives the average person plenty of room to lie down, sleep comfortably and store gear. A tent will also protect from theft because your gear will be out of sight. Additionally, they provide privacy—if more than one person is going on the trip, it may be a good idea for each person to bring their own tent.

There are single-person tents that closely resemble a very large mummy sleeping bag. These tents weigh no

A smaller tent allows you to easily pack up and move to a better site.

REFLECTOR WALL

With any of these shelter variations, you can build a fire in front of the shelter to keep warm. Your shelter will keep the wind and rain off you, but the addition of a fire will keep you from freezing on cold, wet nights. To augment your warmth, you can build a reflector wall for your fire, which will bounce heat toward your shelter and allow you to stay even warmer. A reflector wall can be made by simply piling up rocks or stones, constructing a simple wall with logs or branches or propping up a Mylar blanket. It's a little extra effort, but well worth it for the added comfort.

more than a hammock. They are longer than your body, which allows room for you to store all your gear, and they are an excellent option for someone who doesn't like hammocks. However, they can sometimes be more expensive than a two-person tent.

Canvas tents have been used for hundreds of years, but they're extremely heavy. If you're hiking to a specific location, this tent style will

not make the gear list due to weight alone. However, if you have some conveyance such as an ATV to bring your equipment to a base camp, a canvas tent could be a viable option. With a canvas tent, you can also use a wood-burning stove to cook inside and keep the interior nice and warm. You can add rain protection by hanging a tarp over your tent. To some, this may seem unnecessary as the tent already provides protection from the elements, but this will help prevent water or mud from getting inside. As a wildlife photographer with a camera to take care of, I'm not too fond of the condensation buildup that occurs when sleeping in a tent in the cold. I won't discourage you from using a tent if that's your preference, but for my purpose, I will always choose a hammock or tarp shelter.

COVERING GROUND

With enough high-quality cord, a decent tarp and a little know-how, you can build five types of shelter depending on your needs.

TARPS

ONE OF THE most convenient, useful items when it comes to shelter is the tarp. Tarps are lightweight, highly waterproof, multiuse tools that can be used for everything from serving as shelter itself to making a hammock to collecting and storing drinking water. I use a lightweight, packable tarp practically every time I venture into the woods.

Tarps were first used by sailors hundreds of years ago. Canvas sheets were coated with tar to cover cargo in order to shield it from seawater and the elements. In the 1700s, this same canvas tarp material was used for

soldiers' tents. Advancements were eventually made with oilcloth, making the tarp extraordinarily lightweight, waterproof and portable.

Today, lightweight, waterproof tarps can range in price from a few hundred dollars to just a few bucks at your local department store. The price depends on the material: You get what you pay for.

To use a tarp as a shelter, you will need some variation of cordage (pg. 56) to tie a few knots (pg. 28). But first, you'll need a few sticks to make toggles, which are used as attachment points. Find some sticks approximately the diameter of your pinky finger, then round the ends off and cut each roughly 3 inches long. That's it! Once you have a toggle, you'll soon find that it comes in handy for many other tasks around camp.

FIT FOR THE JOB

Tarps come in various shapes, sizes and configurations, but the one I find myself using the most is the DD 3x3. This tarp measures 3 by 3 meters, or 9.84 by 9.84 feet for those who loathe the metric system. It has 19 attachment points for guylines and stake-downs or tie-outs (which I love) and is completely weather sealed throughout all the stitching—which happens to be double-stitched. In other words, it's a lot more robust than ordinary tarps and is designed for exactly what I purchased it for: camping!

RIDGELINE

A RIDGELINE IS the highest point of your shelter. The term can be used for various types of high-points. Think of a house: The top of the roof where all the rafters tie in is called the ridge. When I make a ridgeline, I use an overhand loop knot on one end of my cordage (pg. 31). Some people use a bowline knot (pg. 33) for when making a ridgeline, but it's merely a matter of preference.

Now that you've made an overhand loop knot, loop your bank line or preferred cordage around the tree. Take your overhand loop knot and slide the long end of your rope (which is called your working end, working part or running end) through the overhand loop. Make a loop to insert your toggle. This end of your ridgeline is now secured to the tree and will not go anywhere until you remove the toggle. Now run your bank line to the other tree.

Next, you'll be making a trucker's hitch. This knot will allow you to tighten your ridgeline and is also used to secure cargo to the roof racks of vehicles or cargo trailers. It's convenient when pulling tension on your rope is necessary.

Start by looping your bank line around the tree.

Next, find a point about 12 to 16 inches from the tree and make a loop in the standing part of the rope. Feed the end of your bank line through the loop and pull it tight, which will make the entire ridgeline very tight.

Pinch the rope where you ran it through the loop and loop the working end around the inside rope twice. Now make another loop, feed your working end through that and leave a tail so that you can quickly disconnect it when you are ready to move your shelter.

I like to set my ridgeline at shoulder height, which is 5 feet for me.

PRUSIK KNOT

TO MAKE ATTACHMENT points for your tarp, You'll need to make two prusik knots. Take your bank line and make an overhand knot; now you have a loop. On your ridgeline, hold your loop up on the back side, loop it around three times and pull it snug. You've just made a Prusik knot.

The Prusik knot allows you to adjust where you want the knot to be, but once you put tension on the knot, it locks into place. Now put another Prusik knot on the other side of the ridgeline. These will be the ridgeline anchor points for the shelter.

QUICK TIP
If you plan to do any mountain climbing on a trip, a Prusik knot is great for gripping a rope.

STAKES

For each of the following shelters, you will need tent stakes or pegs. You can make them from sticks at the campsite or carry some store-bought metal ones. It's easy and convenient to carry four lightweight aluminum stakes, and it's just as easy to make them from fallen limbs. Personally, I like to carry my tent stakes—I often arrive in the woods around nightfall, so I like to set my shelter up first so I can then collect firewood.

Pine boughs, leaves and other soft materials can be used to make a bed.

LEAN-TO SHELTER

OFTEN CONSIDERED THE easiest shelter to make, the lean-to provides shade and decent protection from rain. You will set this shelter up depending on the direction of the wind in order to block its path.

Step 1 Attach one corner of your tarp to your ridgeline by inserting the Prusik loop through the tie-out point and inserting your toggle. Then, do the same on the other side and pull your Prusik loop tight.

Step 2 Go to the back end of your shelter and pull one corner tight and stake it down. Repeat with the other corner.

A-FRAME SHELTER

Step 1 Begin by laying the tarp lengthways across the ridgeline. The ridgeline should be directly in the center of the tarp.

Step 2 Insert your Prusik loop and toggles on both sides (the same way you would with a lean-to), pulling tight.

Step 3 Stake the four corners of the tarp. You now have a shelter that is more protected from wind and rain than a simple lean-to.

If you make your stakes, be sure to use very strong sticks or limbs.

DIAMOND FLY SHELTER

THE DIAMOND FLY is similar to the A-frame in that both are used to cover hammocks but also work well on the ground.

Step 1 Lay your tarp corner to corner over your ridgeline, producing a diamond-like shape.

Step 2 Use the Prusik loop and toggle to anchor the corners to the ridgeline (just like with the A-frame and lean-to shelters) and make it tight on each end.

Step 3 Stake down the two wings, creating a diamond shape that allows for a little more coverage.

A diamond fly takes a little more time but provides more coverage than a lean-to.

ADIRONDACK SHELTER

THE ADIRONDACK SHELTER is traditionally a Three-sided log structure, but you can make one using a tarp. It offers three sides of protection from the elements, making it perfect for colder environments.

Step 1 Lay one corner of the tarp over the ridgeline.

Step 2 Attach a toggle to your tarp by inserting your Prusik loop through the top tie-out point; as you pull on the toggle, the top will get tighter. Attach a toggle to the other end so that there is equal pressure.

Step 3 Go around the back of the tarp and stake down the tie-out points that are directly opposite the toggles. Then tuck the far corner of the tarp underneath; this will give you a small groundsheet.

Step 4 Stake down the two front corner tie-out points, which will create side walls. Flip the leftover top piece back over the ridgeline.

Step 5 Attach a guyline (pg. 96) to the middle of back wall created by the tarp and tie this to another nearby tree. Doing so will create more room inside your shelter.

QUICK TIP

If you build a fire in front of your Adirondack shelter, the heat will be reflected toward your body thanks to the shape and angles of the tarp.

An Adirondack shelter is a great option if you require a more spacious type of shelter.

PLOW POINT SHELTER

THE PLOW POINT is straightforward and can be set up very quickly. This shelter only requires one piece of cordage, and I've even seen them set up without any cordage at all. You do not need a ridgeline for this shelter, you just need at least three stakes to secure your tarp to the ground.

Step 1 Take one corner of the tarp and attach it to a tree over your head (about 7 feet high). The tarp should be hanging in a diamond shape.
Step 2 Pull the farthest end tight and stake it down.
Step 3 Stake down the remaining two corners, pulling tight. That's it! You have created an accessible, fast and very effective shelter.

QUICK TIP
Securing each corner of your shelter with extra stakes is a wise preventative measure.

As its name suggests, this shelter somewhat resembles an old plow

HAMMOCKS

I USUALLY USE A hammock when i camp because of the simplicity and comfort and I'm not eager to sleep on the ground. The only problem with a hammock is finding two trees that are perfectly spaced apart. If the trees are too close, the hammock will sag in the middle, making for an uncomfortable night's sleep. If the trees are too far apart, you have to use extensions ("tree straps," often sold with hammocks) and hang the hammock higher because of sagging, but it will be more comfortable than if the trees were too close.

A hammock can be used with the A-frame and diamond fly. Make a ridgeline about 6 feet high, then make your preferred shelter. If your hammock has a bug net, you may have to make a separate ridgeline for the net. Some newer hammocks allow you to lay flat with a mattress or pad, but I prefer the old-style hammock with a bug net. If you're camping during a cold season, placing an underquilt on the bottom of the hammock will keep you very warm.

When lying in the hammock, you want to be diagonal (see photo). This will eliminate some of the curvature of the hammock, aka the reason some people prefer to sleep in a tent. But when combined with an A-frame or diamond fly, you can still have plenty of room for all your gear and receive just as much protection from the elements as a tent would provide. The only difference between using these two shelter configurations with a hammock is you can't stake the shelter to the ground. You must use guylines

on each corner of your tarp.

Guylines are ropes attached to a fixed point on your tarp, allowing you to tie them farther away. Guyline allows you to make your shelter with a hammock by giving you more length and allowing you to make your cover

broader or narrower, depending on the weather. A typical guyline for use with a hammock is going to be roughly 6 feet. Use an overhand loop knot to attach one end to your tarp tie-out, place a stake in the ground and use the buntline hitch (pg. 32) to secure it. You can even use overhand loop knots on both ends of your guyline, if you prefer. One side is attached to the tarp while the other is around the stake. Finally, use a Prusik knot with a toggle through the other loop end. This creates a very tight guyline that will not slip.

MAKING A SHELTER from natural material is relatively easy; a couple varieties can be made from a sapling and a collection of fallen limbs and leaves. A survival leaf shelter or debris hut can keep you dry in the rain and provide relief from the wind. When coupled with a fire, it creates a micro-environment that can keep you warm, even on freezing nights.

Step 1 Find a sapling at least 8 feet tall that will bend over without breaking. In Mississippi, I like to use a sweet gum tree because it's flexible and bending does not kill it. Once you've selected your sapling, sharpen the top end to a point and push this point into the ground as deep as you can. You should now have an arch made from a live tree. (The tree is not harmed and will continue to grow—once you're done with the shelter, you can disperse the building materials and return the tree to its original position.)

Step 2 Next, gather fallen branches and sticks to lean against one side of the arch. The longer the sticks, the larger the angle you will have for your shelter, allowing more room for you and your gear. Place as many sticks as possible on your arch, closing as many gaps as possible. Use larger branches first, then fill in the remainder with smaller ones. The larger twigs should rest at an angle with one end a few feet away on the ground, the other leaning against the top of the arch; they will act like ceiling joists similar to those in your house. The smaller branches should run horizontally from side to side; this will help trap more debris onto your shelter.

Step 3 Collect lots of leaves to cover all the sticks leaning on the arch. Material used to cover roofs, such as straw, rushes, leaves or the like, is called thatching, and it's used to block the wind and rain and, in hot environments, provide shade from the sun.

To build an A-frame shelter, repeat the steps above (the sapling will have a curve but is still considered an A-frame). An A-frame or opposing lean-to offers more protection and warmth, making it

a better option for colder environments.

Once you've made a natural shelter to camp in, collect more leaves to use as a mattress pad or bedding. This method is best for people who do not have any sheltering system with them.

QUICK TIP

When gathering materials, be wary of snakes and other dangerous animals that might be in the area.

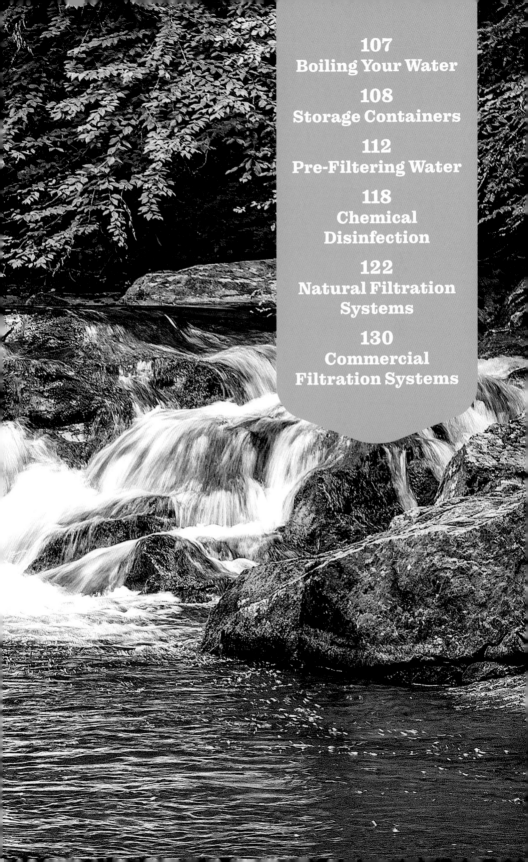

Even if water looks comparatively clean and clear, it should not be consumed until properly purified.

This guide will not go in depth about finding water like other survival books might. The reason is because I assume you are camping in a location with access to a lake, stream, river or even an oak tree that holds water. You can even collect water from a standing puddle found in the woods—standing water in pools near roadways should be avoided, however, due to the higher possibility of contamination from gasoline, motor oil and other chemicals. When finding water in the woods, there are many ways to filter it and make it drinkable. But before you begin those processes, there are many considerations to keep in mind.

Any drinking water derived from surface or groundwater can potentially be contaminated with waterborne pathogens. Most of the time, this is from fecal contamination. Pathogens can originate from sewer and septic systems that have been flooded due to excess rain or river flooding or, in the primitive campers' case, improperly disposed-of waste. Adenovirus, rotavirus, hepatitis A and norovirus are a few viruses of concern. Bacteria are big players in the game as well, including E-coli, Salmonella, Campylobacter and cholera.

Protozoa—such as Cryptosporidium and Giardia—are another type of biological contaminant and carry arguably the most significant risk of illness when camping. Giardia causes the infection giardiasis, also known as "beaver fever." It's one of the most common waterborne illness in the United States. Please note, this is not an exhaustive list of pathogens but rather the most common ones you may encounter while camping. Any of them can cause horrible health symptoms such as gastroenteritis, severe cramping, abdominal pain, dehydration and diarrhea, each of which can last a few days to several weeks. An extreme case of diarrhea that could lead to dehydration is the last thing you want to happen while wandering the woods; it is absolutely no fun.

The scariest culprits you want to be aware of are viruses. Viruses are smaller than bacteria and protozoa, so some can evade filtration. Boiling your drinking water is the safest method of purifying it from these microscopic terrors. Certain protozoa, such as Cryptosporidium and Giardia, are incredibly hardy and can survive other methods like chlorine disinfection. These organisms enter the environment via human and animal waste. Animals such as otters, beavers, deer and moose, to name a few, do not care where they relieve themselves—many of the larger

RAINWATER

Rainwater is safe to drink. Many will argue that rainwater has forever chemicals making it unsafe to drink. If that were truly the case, then all water on Earth would be unsafe to drink, as rivers, lakes, ponds and streams are, for the most part, products of rainwater. PFAS (per-and polyfluoroalkyl substances) are known as forever chemicals because they don't break down in the environment. Forever chemicals are found in numerous consumer goods, including makeup and non-stick pots and pans with a Teflon coating.

Rainwater does not have the biological contaminants that groundwater has and can therefore be collected and consumed without being filtered or boiled. A rain catch can be made from a poncho, tarp, trash bag, plastic sheet or tent rain fly. The easiest to use is a tarp, which you will likely already have set up for your shelter anyway. Simply set up a container to collect the water as it pools or runs off the tarp, then drink as needed or store it for later use.

Rainwater tastes different from water from a stream or lake because it evaporates, leaving behind all the minerals. Once vaporized, the water rises, forms clouds, cools and condenses, turns into rain and falls back to Earth. It is a true example of natural materials being recycled.

critters will feed around lakes, streams and rivers, waist-deep, voiding and defecating at their leisure. This waste then flows downstream to where you are filling up your brand-new squeeze water filter.

Cryptosporidium and Giardia have been found in filtered drinking water supplies and can survive for extended periods. As a general rule, you should boil your drinking water and save the

While rainwater is safe to drink, it may contain debris you'll want to filter out.

personal water filtration system as a last resort. The little invisible things in our water that make us sick are not filtered out like dirt and debris are with a handkerchief or Millbank bag. You will get tired of reading "Boil your water" in this section, but for the sake of safety, it can't be overstated. Boiling your water will disinfect it so that you will not catch any viruses or bacteria

As mentioned in Gear (pg. 40), filtering and purifying water are different processes. Filtering your water removes the sediment, making

it free of grit, grime and other unwelcome guests such as tadpoles and bugs. Purifying your water makes it safe to drink by removing biological pathogens and chemical contaminants.

Chemical contaminants are different from biological pathogens in that chemicals are present in water due to runoff and flooding. For example, a farmer sprays his crops with pesticides, the rain washes the pesticides off the crops and the water collects and runs to a stream. This water is then transported to rivers and so forth. Chemical

E-coli bacteria cells (top) and salmonella bacteria (bottom).

F, and the best way to ensure that you have reached this temperature is to bring your water to a boil. Water boils at 211.9 degrees F (99.97 degrees C) between sea level and 6,500 feet. When boiling your water below 6,500 feet, boil for at least one minute in order to kill the biological pathogens. Above 6,500 feet in elevation, boil the water for at least three minutes. But to be extra safe and ensure your water is free of viruses and other living organisms, boil all water for at least three minutes, regardless of elevation.

Boiling your water will not remove chemical contaminants. Some will evaporate out, but the majority will not. To remove them, you will have to distill your water. This process involves bringing water to a boil, capturing the steam and collecting the condensation as it cools and turns back into water. It is possible to do this with a canteen and nesting cup, but for the most part, you will not have to worry about chemical pollutants when in the woods. The main concern will be biological contaminants.

It takes 45 minutes for freshly boiled water to cool. However, it's possible to cut that time in half if you place the metal container back in the water source. When boiling water straight out of a river or lake, I recommend using a Crystal Light or Wyler's Light packets. These can really help with the taste of the muddy water (especially here in Mississippi). Plus, when camping for an extended period, I sometimes crave Coca-Cola (even though I don't even drink it!), but by using these convenient drink packets, I can avoid wishing I had something to drink other than water.

contaminants are more challenging to eliminate than biological pathogens and have to be removed via different processes than simple filtration. Using a handkerchief (pg. 112) filters water, and boiling purifies it.

BOILING YOUR WATER

Why do we boil water? By boiling your water, you ensure the biological pathogens listed earlier are killed and the water has been disinfected, rendering it safe to drink. Biological contaminants are killed at 165 degrees

Water can easily be boiled on a small camp stove.

and use to boil water. Water can even be boiled in a glass bottle or jar. Still, I can't stress enough how important it is for you to always have some kind of metal container with you. As previously mentioned, I always have a single-walled metal water bottle with me just in case I have to boil water from some stagnant beaver pond—but, once again, *do not use an insulated or double-walled water bottle to boil water.* They can explode!

METAL CONTAINERS

A metal container is one of the most essential items to keep with your gear, alongside your "trusty but not rusty" knife. This item is the most basic way to make water safe to drink, even if you cannot pre-filter it. Any metal container can be used to boil water; and since you're heading to the woods for a camping trip, you should have one on hand to cook with anyway.

If you venture out without packing a metal container, you may still be in luck, as there is hardly any place on Earth that's not touched by human trash. I have been in the mountains far away from civilization and found an aluminum can that I could clean

WATER STORAGE

Water collection bags are readily available, and various retail stores sell them in different quantities and sizes. The 1-gallon size has served me for several years and is perfect for storing both clean and dirty water for later use around camp. I use two bags for clean water and two bags for contaminated water. This gives me 2 gallons of drinkable water and 2 gallons of water to purify when needed. Depending on your environment, you may not need several gallons of water at a time, but you have the option.

Recently, several fast-food restaurants have started selling drinks such as sweet tea or lemonade in reusable 1-gallon bags, which can easily be washed and sanitized for camping. The mouths on these bags tends to be larger and thus cannot be used with the gravity filter system, but you can store contaminated water in them for later

A cookware hanging rack paired with a metal pot is a convenient way to boil your water.

use with your filter. Plus, they typically have the company logo on them so you can easily remember which bag holds the contaminated water and won't accidentally drink from the wrong one. These bags are incredibly lightweight, durable and foldable and can be stowed in your water kit or backpack.

WICKING YOUR WATER

Wicking is the process of a fluid being absorbed or drawn off by capillary action through the fibers of your wick, such as cotton. When wicking water, you are moving it from one place to another. A piece of cotton cloth such as a shemagh, handkerchief or even cotton string can wick dirty water from one container into another. This process will filter the water as it travels the length of the cotton fibers into your collection container. It will be sediment-free, crystal-clear water, but it must still be boiled or passed through a commercial filter (pg. 130) before you drink it.

This process can also be done with two containers, collecting dirty water in one container and wicking it into a clean container. The dirty water container must be elevated slightly higher than the clean container. If this method is used with a handkerchief or bandana, ensure it has been pre-washed; otherwise, the clean water will turn the color of the bandana.

Use both clear and labeled storage bags to differentiate between clean and dirty water.

PRE-FILTERING WATER

Even if you plan to use a commercial filtration system, you should pre-filter your water via one of these processes first.

THE GOOD OLE HANKY

WHEN I WAS A KID, my brother and I went on a camping trip where we decided to go extra minimalist. We only carried 1 pound of dried beans and a #10 tin can for cooking for a four-day trip. We didn't bring any water, only this nifty little pump-style water filter that we had gotten for Christmas. Four hours into our journey, we were thirsty and decided to pump some water. The creek we were going to use as our water source was flooded over the banks—the water is already very sandy and muddy in south Mississippi, and this flooding made the grit and grime even worse. I broke out the little pump water filter and sure enough, it clogged up immediately. It was utterly useless! The only way we could get drinkable water was to boil it and let it cool, so we went to bed thirsty. Later that night, a thunderstorm came through, and we collected rain on our tarp shelters to drink. This taught me a precious lesson. Before you use your handy-dandy store-bought commercial water filter, you still have to pre-filter your water.

Is it possible to find clear and clean water? Absolutely not! All water will have some degree of sediment. Most of the time in Mississippi, the water is tea-stained (brown) and muddy.

The brown color is the result of dead leaves and organic material staining the water as they decompose. In other regions, the water is blue or green and looks milky. This is caused by runoff from the soil, sediment or silt in the water, algae and even minerals released from weathering rocks.

Water can be boiled straight out of a river or stream, but many people prefer to avoid drinking grit. The first step in making your water ready to drink is removing the turbidity (the general cloudiness of a liquid caused by the presence of various particles). Collect water from the cleanest possible source and let it sit for a few minutes until the sediment sinks to the bottom. This is when the cotton hanky works perfectly. This simple filter will remove grit, sticks, bugs and larger particles from the water (but again, it won't remove pathogens). A Millbank bag will also work well for this process; you do not have to let the water sit when using a Millbank bag. Since my first trip into the woods as a kiddo, I've used a cotton handkerchief to remove the grit and grime before filtering or boiling water, and I'll continue to use it on every trip I take.

I have even used a handkerchief to filter the leaves and debris out of my collected rainwater (which was already safe to drink). You can use a cloth or bandana to filter your water into a cup or container or use a few of them to make a tripod filter (pg. 122). Place the bandana over the container's opening, submerge it and allow it to fill up. The deeper the water source, the less debris you will have. Now the water you have collected is ready to boil.

If you don't have a hanky handy, a shemagh can also be used to remove debris.

MILLBANK BAG

RESEMBLING A CHRISTMAS stocking, the Millbank bag is made from heavy, tightly woven canvas and is extremely helpful in getting the grit and debris out of your water. This method is called course filtering in survival and bushcraft circles.

Step 1 Soak the bag in the water for a few minutes to allow the canvas fibers to expand, creating a fantastic water filtration system.

Step 2 Fill it with water and then hang it from a tree. Water will seep through the canvas and drip down to the lowest corner of the bag.

Step 3 Place your metal container under the bag to collect the water. Boil the water or use a commercial filter.

This process will not remove all discoloration, but the water will be free of turbidity. Water with a lot of debris and silt will naturally take longer to filter as the materials you filter out will stick to the inside of the bag, slowing down the process. When this occurs, flip the bag inside out, wash it in your water source, flip it back and continue filtering. Remember, even after filtering with a Millbank bag, you must boil or purify your water.

You can also hang your millbank bag from a cooking spit (pg. 242).

STANDARD COFFEE FILTER

A STANDARD PAPER coffee filter can pre-filter your water like a handkerchief or Millbank bag. The only issue with a coffee filter is that once it becomes wet, it will be hard to manipulate without having some apparatus to keep its form intact. For instance, when you use a coffee pot, the filter and grounds are placed in a brew basket. The brew basket is designed to hold the form of the filter while the hot water pours through the grounds and into the pot. There are funnel-shaped coffee filters that work for pre-filtering water, but they are much more expensive. The best way to maintain a coffee filter's form during pre-filtering is to use a simple rubber band or string to secure the filter around the opening of your container. Then simply pour your dirty water over the filter. Much like the Millbank bag, the more sediment there is in the water, the slower the water will filter.

Experiment with different coffee filters and water containers to find a good combination.

BEYOND A CUP OF MUD

Like many people, I have a Keurig for my coffee needs at home—but instead of using K-cups or pods, I buy regular coffee and use a reusable K-cup coffee filter. One morning while making a cup of coffee, I looked at this filter and realized it could work perfectly for pre-filtering water. So, it was off to the woods to test my theory out. I inserted the filter inside the opening of a 24-ounce aluminum single-walled water bottle and found that it fit perfectly. Just as I suspected, it removed tremendous amounts of sand and debris.

Since that initial experiment, I have found the K-cup coffee filter to be perfect for filtering out grit, grime and extra protein like tadpoles and bugs. It will give you the cleanest possible dirty water to boil or use with your commercial water filter. Plus, if you bring coffee, you also have the added benefit of using it to make your next cup of joe.

CHEMICAL DISINFECTION

If you have used either a handkerchief, Millbank bag or coffee filter and you do not have a commercial filter, you can use chemical disinfection.

TABLETS

Various chemical disinfectants, such as chlorine and iodine, are on the market today, and the Potable Aqua iodine tablets pictured here are available in nearly all sporting goods stores. As a disclaimer, you should try to limit the use of this method as much as possible. I only use this method and any other chemical decontamination process covered in this chapter as a last resort. According to *WebMD*, prolonged iodine use might exacerbate thyroid disorders such as hypothyroidism and may also cause upset stomach and sore teeth and gums.

Packs of Potable Aqua also include

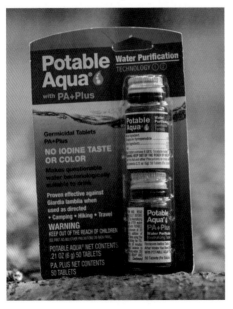

neutralizing tablets to eliminate the taste of iodine. Use two neutralizing tablets and wait three minutes before drinking. The neutralizing tablets do not have to be completely dissolved before consumption.

10 PERCENT POVIDONE-IODINE (BETADINE) PURIFICATION

Iodine kills biological pathogens such as Giardia, bacteria and viruses as effectively as chlorine bleach, but it carries a greater risk. Iodine should not be used for prolonged periods or by people who are pregnant or have thyroid problems. With that in mind, research by the CDC, EPA, NIH, WHO and FEMA has proven that iodine is an effective way to disinfect water from biological contaminants.

Once again, before beginning this purification process, pre-filter your water with a handkerchief, Millbank bag or coffee filter. If you don't have a way to pre-filter the water, allow the water to settle until all the sediment has sunk to the bottom of your container, then pour the clear water into another container.

Step 1 If the water is cold and cloudy, add 14 drops of iodine per liter. For clear warm water, add 7 drops. For example, if I used clear water from a pond on a warm day and the water temperature was near the 70s, I would use 7 drops. If the water was from a

The hanky is one of the most useful items across all water filtering and purification processes.

A medicine bottle with a dropper is perfect for measuring bleach and iodine by the drop. It's small, lightweight and easy to carry.

river and was cold and cloudy, I would use 14 drops.

Step 2 Shake or stir the container. Let stand for 15–20 minutes before drinking.

Step 3 To combat the unpleasant taste of water treated with iodine, use a vitamin C tablet or lozenge. Or, use a drink packet as mentioned on pg. 203.

BLEACH PURIFICATION

Drinking water can be rendered safe by using unscented household chlorine bleach. Bleach can kill most harmful or disease-causing viruses and bacteria, but it is not as effective as boiling for destroying germs such as Cryptosporidium and Giardia. Water contaminated with other chemicals can't be disinfected with bleach.

Before purifying with bleach, pre-filter your water with a handkerchief, Millbank bag or coffee filter. If you do not have a way to pre-filter the water, allow the water to settle until all the sediment has sunk to the bottom of your container. Then pour the clear water into another container.

Use unscented household liquid chlorine bleach with a 5–9 percent sodium hypochlorite concentration (*do not* use scented or concentrated bleach). These concentrations are most common in the United States and may differ in other countries.

CONCENTRATION CALCULATIONS

For concentrations of bleach within the United States that use 5–9 percent sodium hypochlorite:

- For 1 liter of water, add 2 drops of bleach.
- For 1 gallon of water, add 8 drops of bleach.
- For 5 gallons of water, add 40 drops of bleach.

If the water is cloudy, colored or very cold, double the amounts of bleach listed above. Stir or shake the container well and let sit for 30 minutes before drinking.

For concentrations of bleach typically found outside the United States that use 1 percent sodium hypochlorite:

- For 1 liter of water, add 10 drops of bleach.
- For 1 gallon of water, add 40 drops of bleach.
- For 5 gallons of water, add 200 drops of bleach.

Once again, if the water is cloudy, colored or very cold, double the amounts of bleach listed above. Stir or shake the container well and let sit for 30 minutes before drinking.

NATURAL FILTRATION SYSTEMS

Mother Nature provides plenty of ways to filter your water, as long as you're willing to put in a little extra effort.

TRIPOD FILTER

THIS WATER FILTRATION system is frequently found in standard survival handbooks, and I first tried making one after seeing it in a survival book myself. It worked exceptionally well. The principles of the tripod water filter are the same as the bottle filter on pg. 128, and everything you need can be found in the natural environment, except the handkerchiefs. The idea behind this filter is to create layers for your water to filter through. The top layer contains grass or small rocks (whichever you have access to), the middle layer has charcoal and the bottom layer has sand. This is a little backward from what you may have seen in some survival books because water tends to turn muddy or milky when charcoal is the bottom layer. If you put the charcoal before the sand, the sand filters the charcoal dust and clears the water. Keep in mind, though—clear water does not mean safe-to-drink water; it merely means the water is free of decomposed leaves, grit, algae and anything else that discolors it.

To build a tripod water filter, you first need to build a tripod. It is very simple and can also be used for cooking and smoking various foods over a campfire (pg. 238).

Step 1 Cut three equal-length (and as straight as possible) sticks approximately 6 feet long. Lay the sticks down and loosely tie some bank line or paracord loop around all three sticks on one end.

Step 2 Flip the middle stick 180 degrees. This will tighten the cordage around the tripod, and you will not have to lash it together.

Step 3 Tie the first handkerchief to each leg near the tripod's top. Drop down 16 inches and secure your next handkerchief. Repeat for the last one.

But if a tripod has three legs and a handkerchief has four corners, how do you secure the handkerchief? This is a question I often receive in the comments on my videos, and the answer is straightforward. Use a rock, some dirt, an acorn or a stick to fold under the fourth corner. Use bank line to tie an overhand loop knot or a jam knot into the fabric behind the object you used. This will give you more of a triangle shape for tying your handkerchief to the tripod and allow you to center all your stages.

In the top layer of the filter, use grass or small pebbles to collect larger debris. You might question why you would put anything in this layer since the handkerchief filters the big stuff out anyway. While this is true (making the contents of this layer optional), I recommend it because large debris

will stick to the grass or pebbles and prevent the cloth from clogging.

The middle layer is the most time-consuming because you must make charred material or charcoal—be prepared to get a little dirty. Charcoal isn't hard to make; simply take logs out of your fire and scrape the black char into a handkerchief. You want a sizable amount to effectively filter the water. The charcoal makes the water taste a lot cleaner and more refreshing. The charred material will absorb some pathogens and contaminants, but not all.

The bottom layer tends to raise the most questions from viewers. Comments generally range from "Where do I find the sand?" to "I'm not going to carry 25 pounds of sand with me!" Sand can be locally sourced from a creek, river, stream, lake or wherever there is water, especially in the southeastern United States. While hiking in north Georgia, I found sand in streams running through the hills. Not all sand you find will be like the beautiful white sand on the beaches of Florida or California; it will be tiny pulverized rocks, especially in mountainous terrain or hilly country. For the purpose of this filter, these crushed rocks are small enough to do the trick.

Fill the top of your filter with water and watch the water pour through each stage. Place a metal pot on the ground to collect your filtered water. After you have run the water through the filter, pour it back in. You may have to do this several times before the water comes out clear. Once you have clear water, boil it or use your commercial filter to make it safe to drink.

QUICK TIP

If your tripod is sturdy enough, you can also use it to make a bushcraft recliner.

You won't find perfectly straight sticks, so just get as close as possible.

COYOTE WATER WELL

THE COYOTE WATER well, also known as a seep well, has been used for ages, from pioneers to modern-day survivalists. This type of well has helped me several times on day trips and is relatively easy to make. The premise behind it is to let nature filter your water.

Step 1 Dig a hole 3 feet away from your water source. The water will filter through all the natural sand and clay into your hole and gradually become cleaner.

Step 2 If there is sand near the water source, such as a sand bar, dig your hole 8 feet away. Once water fills the well, let the sediment clear and scoop your water into a container.

Step 3 Once you've gathered your water, boil it or use your commercial filter to make it safe to drink. This water generally has a lower chance of being contaminated with biological pathogens, but as with anything outdoors, there is always some risk. Best to be on the safe side.

Water filtration systems will not filter out salt from salt water. Making salt water drinkable is an entirely different process called desalination.

THE BOTTLE FILTER involves the same process as the tripod filter but in a self-contained system. The most common (and most easily found) bottle to use is a 2-liter soda bottle.

Step 1 Tie a handkerchief, coffee filter or cloth around the opening or mouth of the bottle.

Step 2 Cut off the bottom or "butt" of the bottle. Flip the bottle mouth-side down.

Step 3 Fill the bottom third of the bottle with sand. Layer a few inches of charcoal and fill the top with pebbles or more sand if you do not have pebbles. You can even use grass at the top of the filter, like in the tripod.

Step 4 Cut a hole in each side at the top of the filter and run a length of bank line or paracord through so it can hang from a tree branch. Run water through the filter and collect it in a

metal container. Like before, you may need to run it through the filter a few times before the water comes out clear.

Remember, clear does not mean it's safe to drink! Boil the water or use your commercial water filter.

While any large plastic bottle will work, a clear bottle allows you to easily see each layer as you build the filter.

QUICK TIP
Once removed, the bottom of the plastic bottle can be used as a cup or bowl.

COMMERCIAL FILTRATION SYSTEMS

If you're looking for a little more convenience when it comes to your water needs, there are many filter options on the market.

WELCOME TO A new rabbit hole! There are countless personal water filters on the market today and each claims to be the best. They all do the same thing: make dirty water drinkable. You do not have to boil water with these water filtration systems, but you should still pre-filter your water to extend the life of your filter and prevent health risks.

Commercial water filters have a medium or cartridge, usually made from ceramic or fiberglass material, that filters the water. This media is porous enough to allow water to pass through but the pores are small enough to trap bacteria, viruses and protozoa. Some variations of these filters contain carbon or charcoal to absorb some pathogens and improve the taste of the water. A commercial water filter coerces the water through the media via pumping, squeezing, sucking or gravity.

Squeeze filters are compact, making them good to carry as a backup in case your preferred filter fails.

PUMP FILTER

PUMP FILTERS HAVE an input tube and an output tube and feature a pumping mechanism such as palm pump, rotary pump or push pump. The input tube is placed into the water source; the pumping mechanism then sucks the water from the source and deposits it into a clean container. It takes a little work, but you can produce large quantities for multiple people. If you aren't careful about where your input tube is placed, however, you might suck up plenty of dirt and clog the filter.

GRAVITY FILTER

GRAVITY FILTERS ARE one of my go-to items thanks to their simplicity: The dirty water reservoir can be filled with 6 liters of water then hung up to let gravity do its job. It filters all the drinking water needed for my entire trip. I have even made a closed system variation of this filter from a 1-gallon water storage bag. Fill the dirty bag, hang it up and let it drain into the clean bag while doing chores around camp. It's effortless and allows me to multitask without worrying about water.

A gravity filter can be modified using storage bags such as those on pg. 111.

Hang your gravity filter from a sturdy branch on a tree close to camp.

The squeeze filter has the advantage of being easy to use on the go.

SQUEEZE FILTER

SQUEEZE FILTERS ARE ubiquitous among hikers and backpackers. They typically come with a 16-to-24-ounce bag that you fill with water. After screwing the filter media onto the bag, you can safely squeeze the water into your container or mouth. I began my commercial filter journey with the squeeze filter, and I still have one in my backpack every time I venture out. They are easy to use, reliable as long as you pre-filter your water and can be backwashed once you return from your trip, extending the filter's life.

QUICK TIP

Using a smartwater bottle attached to your squeeze filter can help lighten the load and serve more than one purpose (pg. 178).

LOOK INTO THE LIFESPAN

Over the years, I have employed countless commercial gravity-fed water filters, which work great initially. But all commercial water filters have the same problem: The filter clogs with mud, debris and sediment. Some filters come with a giant syringe to backwash and remove the grit and debris when you return home and have access to clean water, and some even hook up to a garden hose for backwashing. This process is very efficient, but eventually, your filter will permanently clog regardless of how much you backwash it. All commercial water filtration systems are rated for a limited number of gallons they will effectively filter over their lifetime. This rating is accurate even if you backwash your filter system after each use.

The LifeStraw is advertised as having "no shelf life" but should still be cared for as you would other filters.

STRAW FILTER

STRAW FILTERS ARE widespread and well-known among outdoor enthusiasts, particularly the LifeStraw water filter. I have one in my water kit, hunting kit and boating kit. These are so cost-effective that you can sometimes buy a pack of five for the price of one squeeze filter system. Straw filters are perfect for when you need water ASAP. Many gravity filter systems use the straw filter for the entire system, and various bladder bags you can purchase for your backpack can implement an in-line straw filter to filter dirty water on demand as you hike.

QUICK TIP

Do not use your water filter if it has frozen. The freezing water will crack or break the filter media and render it useless.

MY FAVORITE FILTER

The commercial filter I personally use whenever I venture outdoors is the Grayl GeoPress. It has become the go-to filter system of countless outdoors enthusiasts, bushcrafters and survivalists, many of whom consider it to be one of the absolute best filtration systems on the market. It has four parts: the cap or lid, the inner press, a replaceable filter cartridge and the outer cup. To use one, you simply fill the outer cup to the fill line, insert the inner press, unscrew the cap and push the water press down. The inner press will fill up, and within eight to 11 seconds, you will have 24 ounces of purified water ready to drink.

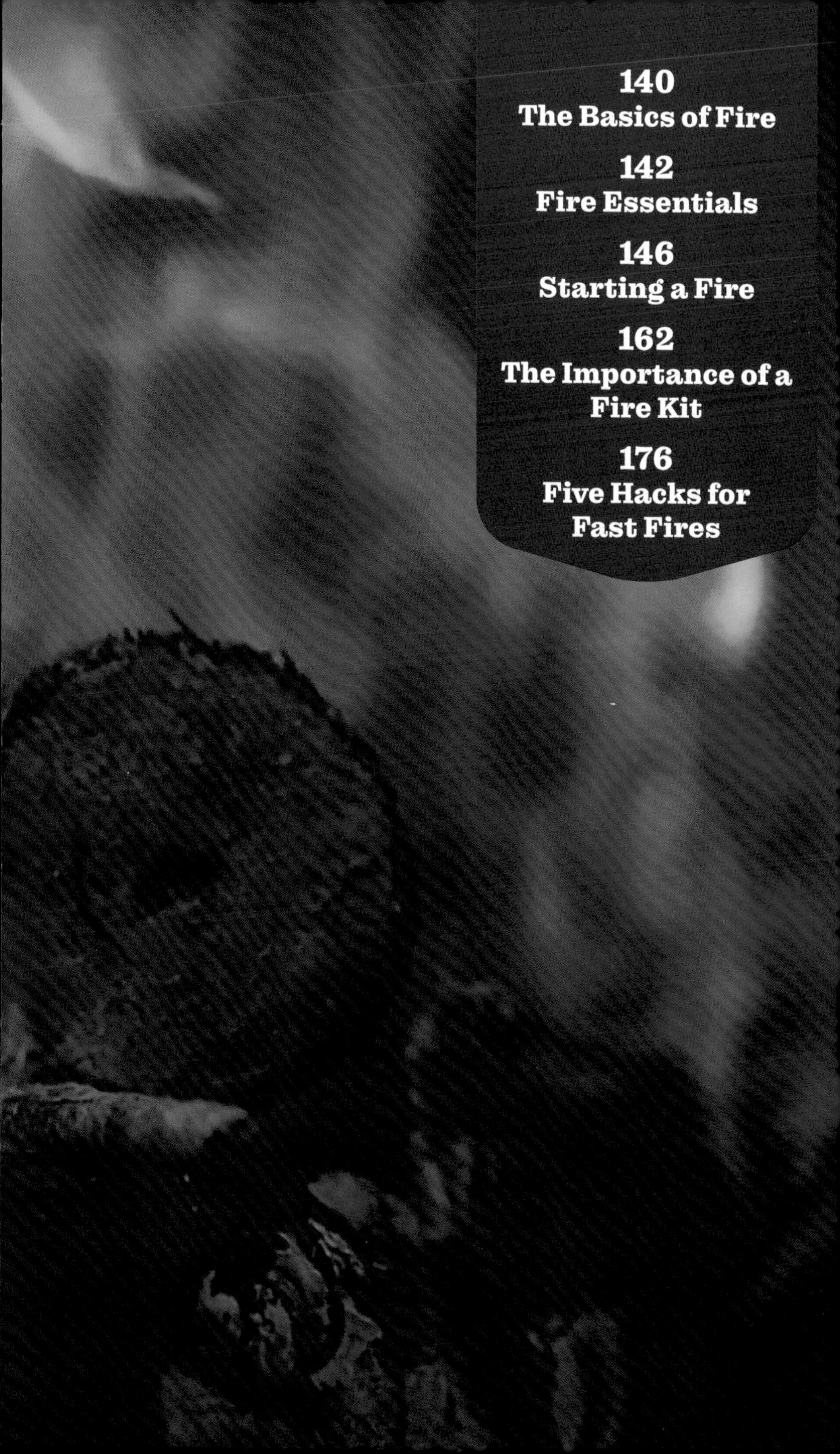

A good campfire is often called "the television of the woods." Beyond providing you with entertainment and relaxation, a fire can also cook your food, boil your water and even save your life. I have spent many hours in the woods coming up with new camping hacks while simply sitting and watching a fire with utter amazement. If you ask any survivalist, they will tell you there is no universal way to start a fire—there are plenty of effective methods. But, if you're not prepared and don't understand the components of fire, starting one can be a challenging, frustrating endeavor.

Never leave a campfire unattended—even a small fire can get out of hand in no time.

FIRE ESSENTIALS

FIRE IS DEFINED as the phenomenon of combustion giving off heat and light from a flame. What does that mean? Think of fire as a triangle: On top, you have heat, and on the bottom corners, you have oxygen and fuel. When all three components are combined, you have a fire.

Oxygen is necessary for the fuel to burn and thus must always be present during all stages of fire building and maintenance. To put it another way, if a fire can't breathe, it dies. The air around us is approximately 20 percent oxygen, and when we inhale we only use a portion of that oxygen. When we blow on a fire, we're exhaling all that unused oxygen—which the fire then consumes as it grows. This remaining oxygen is why a fire grows when we blow on the coal to bring it to flame.

Fire must have something combustible to keep the flames alive. The combustible element is divided into three additional components—tinder, kindling and fuel.

TINDER

Tinder is any material (natural or artificial) that can light with a spark. This material is usually folded together like a bird's nest to catch the spark and

KINDLING

TINDER

initiate combustion. The material you select as tinder should be made from thin wood shavings or very fine natural or artificial fibers. There are numerous types of tinder within the natural environment, such as dogfennel. A perennial weed found in the southeastern U.S., dogfennel produces small flowers in the late fall, which then die and dry out over the winter. When spring comes around, these flowers make one of the most amazing types of tinder you can find. Additionally, many other natural materials such as goldenrod and other common weeds are equally effective as tinder.

Depending on your environment or geographic location, there may be other natural materials available for tinder. The key is to practice with different materials before you go out in the wild—

TINDER FROM GREEN WOOD

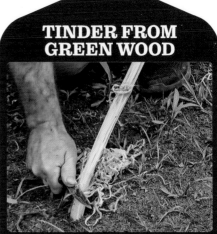

When I first saw someone on YouTube use an arrowwood shrub as tinder, it blew my mind! This went against everything I knew about fire at the time. Bark from a green limb is saturated with water—usually, the only way to dry it out is by letting it sit for days. With arrowwood, however, that's not the case. You can make shavings and place them in direct sunlight, where they will dry quickly. If you're ever in a desperate situation and an arrowwood shrub is all you can find, here's how this green wood can help you start a fire.

1. Once you identify an arrowwood shrub, cut off a section about 2 feet long.

2. Scrape off the outer bark and set it aside for the fire. You should be left with a yellowish stick.

3. Using the 90-degree spine on the back of your knife blade, start scraping the stick's length to get nice long shavings. Keep doing this around the stick until you have a huge pile of tinder.

4. Set the shavings in the sun for about 20 minutes to dry. Next, take your ferro rod and strike the rod into the fresh pile of tinder. It may take a few strikes, but eventually, you will start a fire.

FUEL

You can never have too much kindling on hand.

by attempting to light various weeds and flowers, you'll know what to look for if you end up needing alternative tinder. Artificial fire tinder such as homemade fire biscuits (pg. 174) wet fire, tinder wick and hemp rope can also be carried in your fire kit (pg. 162), which should be lightweight and easily stowed in your pack. I recommend you take it with you on any outdoor adventure.

The options are endless when it comes to natural tinder. Dry grasses, dry leaves, pine needles, weeds, cattail fluff, bark from various types of trees—any tinder you decide to use (natural or artificial) will lay a foundation for you to generate a spark and easily create a small flame that will then be kindled into a bigger fire.

KINDLING

Kindling is an elementary part of a fire. I have used kindling as the only fuel for many of my wood-burning stoves. It's readily available and, depending on location, extremely plentiful. Essentially, kindling is small dead twigs. When smaller trees get choked out and die, they become easy targets for fire kindling—you can always find dead limbs or sticks that have fallen from a tree and are hanging from the tops of small trees or vines. These will be dryer than the material on the ground, so just grab what you find and break it up to add to your tinder when you're ready to start your fire.

FEATHER STICKS

FUEL

The final component of fire, fuel, is the large items that burn and keep the fire going—hopefully for hours on end! Large, split logs (like those used for a fireplace) are the most common and effective form of fuel. You want to be as prepared as possible to keep feeding the fire, so be sure to bring a quality axe or saw (pg. 53) and stock up beforehand.

Ash, maple, birch, oak and hickory are among the many types of wood that work well as fire fuel. The availability of these trees will of course depend on location. And much like with tinder, it doesn't hurt to experiment with using different types of wood as fuel to see which burns best.

If you're dealing with wet logs or sticks, you can still have dry kindling by making a feather stick.

1. Find a log roughly 2 to 3 inches in diameter and split it in quarters to create four pie-shaped sticks.

2. Holding your knife still, pull one of the sticks along the blade to make a thin shaving all the way down the stick. Once you have gotten close to the end of the stick, repeat the process as many times as necessary until you have made the stick look like the vane of a feather.

By making these thin strips on the stick, you are creating more material for the fire to consume as it grows. This method is extremely useful when you're camping in a wet environment. An alternative way to make these shavings is to lodge your knife into a log and then pull the stick against the knife.

STARTING A FIRE

Now that you know the elements required, it's time to put them to use to create your own flames.

IN GENERAL, IF you have dry tinder, kindling and fuel as well as a simple lighter, getting a fire going is a fairly straightforward endeavor. But life (especially in a survival camping setting) isn't always straightforward. That's why it's helpful to know how to build a fire under even the most extreme conditions.

There are many ways to apply heat when building a fire. You can use friction from a bow drill, flint or steel, a spark from a ferro rod, or even magnified light from the sun via a magnifying glass or plastic water bottle. Once your generated spark (or heat) is transferred into your tinder bundle and given oxygen, you will have a flame. This flame will then ignite your kindling, to which you will gradually and continuously add fuel.

FLINT AND STEEL

IN EARLY HISTORY, prior to the development of steel, flint and iron pyrite (commonly known as fool's gold) were forcefully struck together to create sparks for fires. Eventually, pyrite was replaced by metal strikers fashioned in "D" or "C" shapes that easily fit around two or three fingers. These metal strikers, when paired with a sharp edge of flint, quartz or chert, create hot sparks when struck—an innovation that forever changed the way we make fire in the wilderness.

When you pair the flint and steel with a material called char cloth, you can quickly catch an ember onto the char cloth, which can then be transferred to your tinder and blown into flame. Hold the sharp edge of your stone at roughly 45 degrees in one hand, take the striker in the other hand and hit it against the stone in a rolling motion. You're not trying to chip the rock but rather scrape metal shavings off the striker. When rapidly oxidized by striking the stone, hot sparks then ignite the char cloth.

You can usually get around 10,000 uses out of a steel striker, depending on its quality.

FERRO ROD

THE FERROCERIUM ROD, better known as the ferro rod, has been used since the early 1900s and has become a go-to fire-starting tool for survivalists and bushcrafters worldwide. In 1903, ferrocerium alloy was invented by the Austrian chemist Carl Auer von Welsbach. Ferrocerium is a synthetic pyrophoric (any material liable to ignite spontaneously on exposure to oxygen) alloy blended with cerium, iron and magnesium. When a ferro rod is struck with a hard material, such as the 90-degree spine of a knife, fragments of the rod are scraped off and exposed to oxygen in the air, igniting the pieces via friction. These scrapings become hot sparks reaching 5,430 degrees Fahrenheit, which can easily ignite a diverse assortment of tinder, from dry grasses and pine needles to wood shavings.

This ease of flammability gives ferrocerium many commercial applications. It can be found in cigarette lighters, strikers for gas welding and cutting torches. Ferro rods come in many shapes and sizes, with diameters ranging from 1 inch to $1/32$ of an inch or smaller in modern cigarette lighters. Some survival kits feature ferro rods attached to survival bracelets, necklaces and keychains.

Many ferro rods come with a striker tied to the rod with either a leather strap or paracord. To use the included striker, place your tinder where you want to ignite it (usually on a solid surface). Firmly place your rod on the edge of the tinder and scrape the rod

When using the included striker, strike directly onto the tinder.

Practice both options for holding the knife to find what works best for you.

a few times back and forth until the tinder ignites.

When using a knife, you can strike the ferro rod in two different ways: Holding the knife stationary and upside down (sharp side up) where the 90-degree spine is facing the rod while scraping material off the rod into the tinder or holding the knife stationary with the 90-degree spine facing up and pulling the rod against the top of the knife to remove the ferrocerium. Either way takes a little practice to become proficient.

Option 1

Hold your knife upside down (sharp side facing up) with the spine facing toward the ferro rod. Hold your hands close enough to your tinder for the sparks to land in it. Pull the rod back against your knife. If you're not able to start a fire after several strikes, reassess your tinder source.

Option 2

Turn the knife right side up (sharp side down) and do the same process. Hold the knife at the edge of your tinder and pull the ferro rod back across the spine of the knife. Remember, it's OK if the tinder does not ignite on the first try; keep repeating the process until you succeed. Practice with different types of tinder and find out which ones ignite faster.

You may notice your ferro rod developing ridges or bumps where you have previously scraped it. This is caused by not applying steady pressure down the length of your rod while striking it. These bumps can easily be filed off. As you continue to practice making steady strokes down the ferro rod, you'll likely notice fewer ridges and bumps developing.

From left: the bow, the spindle, the hearth board and the bearing block (coal catch not pictured).

BOW DRILL

TYPICALLY, WHEN PEOPLE think about starting a fire with natural materials, they picture rubbing two sticks together. Whether they know it or not, the method they're thinking of is known as the bow drill. This method has been used since man's earliest ventures in making fire and remains a viable option today.

Once you know how to put together a bow drill set, a bit of practice (believe me, it takes a good bit) will allow you to start a friction fire in just a few minutes. Still, it's not as easy as some people make it look—I have filmed both my failures and successes. To be

transparent, I was utterly exhausted after starting my first bow drill fire. Even though I managed to make a fire, my technique was incorrect. And that's the thing: The bow drill requires proper technique and a fair amount of patience. You cannot rush the process.

A bow drill is made up of four parts: the hearth board, bearing block, spindle or drill and bow. You want to make the hearth board and spindle from the same type of softwood. The bearing block can be made from hardwood or fatwood (resinous wood filled with pine sap, see pg. 176), and the bow can be made from any wood.

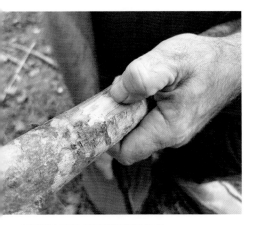

QUICK TIP
You may have to look a bit beyond your campsite to find ideal materials, but it will be worth the hike.

branches on the ground, which are more prone to rotting.

HEARTH BOARD

Find a branch or stick 2 inches or slightly larger in diameter. With your saw or knife, cut it so it's about the length of your forearm, from elbow to fingertips. Use a knife to cut it roughly 1 inch thick. Then use a mallet (any log or branch) to hammer your knife through the length of the wood. This method is called batoning. Do the same thing on the other side. Using your knife, shave the board on both sides to make it nice and flat. It should now resemble a small piece of lumber ubiquitous at hardware stores.

FINDING MATERIALS

To find the right wood, use your knife to scrape some bark off the wood you intend to use. In the shaved area, press your thumbnail into the wood. If it leaves a deep indentation, you have found a softwood that will generally work for a bow drill. If it only leaves a shallow indentation, you've found hardwood, which will still work for the bearing block. I usually look for a standing dead tree because the wood is generally more durable than fallen

For safety and efficiency, be sure your knife is sharpened before making the hearth board.

Determine the length
before shaving the bark.

SPINDLE

Select a branch from the same tree or wood from which you created your hearth board, about the diameter of your thumb and roughly 8-12 inches long (a common method for finding a good spindle length is to open your hand and use the distance from the tip of the pinky finger to the tip of your thumb). Using your knife, shave off all the bark and smooth out any knots and bumps. Once completed, it should look like a short, fat dowel rod. On one end, carve a point like you're sharpening a pencil. Round off the other end to resemble a pencil eraser.

QUICK TIP

If materials are scarce, the spindle can be made from a harder wood than the hearth board.

If possible, find a branch without many knots and bumps to simplify things.

BOW

For the bow, you'll need a strong stick slightly thicker than your thumb's diameter. I prefer a green sapling and often use the Chinese privet, which is plentiful in south Mississippi and grows with a natural arch. Some primitive campers prefer to use a straight stick, but I like my bows to have a slight curve. When I use a straight stick, my hand sometimes hits the spindle. The length of your bow should be approximately 3 feet or one arm's length, which you can determine by measuring the distance from the top of your shoulder to your fingertips. Use paracord or tarred and twisted bank line for your bowstring.

You may need to make several string adjustments before finding the right tension.

If you don't have any cordage for your bowstring, you can use a shoelace.

To attach your bowstring, use a folding saw to cut a slit roughly 1 inch deep in both ends of the bow. Take your cordage, tie an overhand knot into it and slide the cordage through the slit at one end. Then, putting a little tension on the bow, do the same for the other end. When you release the bow, you have just the right amount of stress on the string. Doing this will allow you to wrap your string or cordage around your spindle and make everything tight enough to operate the bow drill.

BEARING BLOCK

For the bearing block, use green hardwood, resinous fatwood or stone or metal with a small divot (many newer flint and steel sets have a divot just for this purpose). Some modern survival knives have divots in the handles specifically for bow drills. Your bearing block should be the width of your hand and roughly the same diameter as the stick you found for the

hearth board. All you need to do is split it down the center and use your knife to create a divot in the center. That's it. The bearing block is the easiest part of the entire operation.

HEARTH BOARD SOCKET AND DIVOT

Now it's time to prepare your hearth board. Place your spindle on the point where you want to make your

Cut the divot in the hearth board slowly to avoid creating a larger hole than you need.

BURN-IN

Now it's time for the process known as the burn-in. You will need something under the board to capture all the dust placed (this is called a coal catch). I typically use a large leaf, but you can use bark or anything else you have handy.

Wrap the bowstring around the spindle, carefully lay the spindle against the string and twist it until the line wraps around the spindle one time. Place one foot on top of the hearth board to hold it steady. With your bearing block in hand, place the spindle in the hearth board socket and set the bearing block on top of the spindle. Add slight downward pressure to the spindle via the bearing block and begin to move the bow back and forth. The goal is to mate the spindle to the socket. Slowly and steadily add pressure as you move the bow back and forth until you see smoke.

socket. Twist it a few times to leave an impression in the board. The socket should be slightly off-center from the board and approximately ½ to ¾ of an inch from the edge. Take your knife and cut a divot into the board where you created the impression. It does not have to be a huge hole but rather a nice little seat for the spindle to sit in.

"V" NOTCH

Once you see smoke, the burn-in process is complete and it's time to add the "V" notch to the hearth board. The "V" notch is where the dust collects from the spindle and hearth board. This dust will build up until the friction ignites it and an ember or coal is formed. Then you will start your fire by transferring the coal into the tinder bundle and giving it oxygen until it ignites.

Take the hearth board and cut a notch in the shape of a "V." This notch will extend from the outer edge of the board to nearly an $\frac{1}{8}$ of an inch into the divot. This step can be done with a knife but is much easier with a saw.

Flip the board over and carve an angle into the bottom portion of the notch. Doing this will allow more oxygen to reach the ember once it starts combustion.

MAKING SMOKE

Place your foot close to the socket for stability. As you did for the burn-in portion, insert the spindle into the socket and place the bearing block on top. Lean forward slightly and rest the hand holding the block on your shin to keep it stable.

Slowly and steadily start moving the bow, applying steady downward pressure. If the string is slipping, you are adding too much pressure. Slowly move the bow back and forth until the "V" notch has filled with dust, at which point you can begin to operate the bow faster while adding more pressure. Once you see smoke, keep going; do not stop until you see a steady stream of smoke from the pile of dust in the "V" notch.

At this point, your ember should be smoking quite a bit. Slowly and gently tilt your hearth board and tap the ember dust out. You may see the ember glowing bright orange at this point. Grab your tinder bundle and carefully transfer the ember into your bundle. Raise the bundle and blow onto the ember, slow and steady.

Start blowing gently—the more smoke you see, the harder you will blow.

Blowing slowly will allow the coal to grow hotter—as you start to see more smoke, gradually blow harder to feed the coal plenty of oxygen, allowing it to rupture into flame.

BLOWING EMBER OR COAL INTO FLAME

When you start a fire outdoors, especially using primitive methods, you will often start with an ember or coal, which you will slowly blow into flame. Since you're essentially putting your face near a soon-to-be fire, caution is required. As you blow, be careful not to get too close to the flames, especially if you have facial hair—this may seem like common sense, but many people overlook this basic step.

SHOTGUN SHELL BOW DRILL

IF YOU WERE venturing into the woods for the sole purpose of hunting, you likely wouldn't carry a lot of survival or bushcraft gear. Realistically speaking, most hunters do not travel so far into the woods that they cannot find their way out, but on the off chance that this did occur—say your compass broke or your GPS battery died—would you be able to start a fire to keep yourself warm until you could find your way out? Imagine that in addition to your navigation gear failing, you also realize you didn't pack a lighter. Now you'll need to get more creative when it comes to starting a fire. Fortunately, you can make what's known as a shotgun bow drill using some materials you likely have on hand.

A belt knife (which I personally always—and I mean always—carry with me in the woods) can be used to make a bow drill set as detailed on pg. 150, and all the steps are essentially the same.

Before you begin to make a shotgun shell bow drill, make sure you have ample tinder, kindling and fuel to create a successful fire on the first go as this may be your only chance of starting one.

You will not cut a "V" notch in the hearth board; instead, you will carve a trail leading from the socket to the end of the board. Then, hold your shotgun shell up to a light source—you should see a clear space between the shot and the wad and powder area. Make your cut in this area to open the shell, then carefully sprinkle the socket and the trail with gunpowder.

Lay your tinder on the ground with the hearth board on top to hold it in place and sprinkle a little gunpowder inside the bundle. Operate the bow drill in the same manner detailed on pg. 157, and when you see smoke, it should ignite the gunpowder, which in turn will ignite the tinder.

Be cautious: Spilled gunpowder can ignite elsewhere and cause an unwanted fire.

Use your knife to carefully cut into the shotgun shell and open it up.

The Importance of a
FIRE KIT

A FIRE KIT is a collection of items that can be used to start a fire, and the size of this kit can vary depending on how comfortable you are with starting primitive fires in the woods. I like my fire kit to encompass various methods for starting a fire. For the kit itself, I use a canvas bag from a hobby store that I waxed to make it water resistant.

Fire kits do not have to be complicated or include 30 different methods to start a fire. Concentrate on easy methods you can use in case your lighter runs out of fluid or you lose your ferro rod. Always make sure you get out and practice with every item in your kit to ensure you're highly proficient at starting a fire with all the options at your disposal. Remember, fire is an important tool. It regulates your body temperature, boils your water, cooks your food and gives you light at night. Make sure you have a way to start a fire regardless of the situation, tinder and environmental factors.

BIC LIGHTER

The Bic lighter is the single most cost-effective and reliable way to start a fire. Other brands are nice, and I'm not endorsing the company, but the product speaks for itself. Always select a brightly colored lighter so it's easy to spot if you drop it. Keep in mind that a Bic lighter will not operate in below-freezing temperatures, so you have to keep it warm. It also won't work when wet, but you can simply dry it off to get it throwing flames again in no time. Remember the old saying: "Two is one, and one is none." When camping or hiking, keep one lighter on your person, one in your fire kit and one in your backpack. This way, you have a backup to the backup.

Before heading out on a trip, I recommend modifying your Bic lighter(s) by removing the metal child safety ring. When your hands are cold and you lose dexterity, it becomes difficult to depress this little metal ring and turn the striker wheel simultaneously.

Here's another tip: Wrap duct tape around the lighter for later use. The tape can have many uses, one of which is to start a fire. Rip off a strip of duct tape from your lighter, put it in on your tinder and light it. This will make the fire burn longer and give you a better chance of igniting your tinder. I have seen other experienced campers wrap jute twine or

bank line around the lighter, which has a similar effect.

CHAR CLOTH

Char cloth is essentially a small-scale variation of charcoal. This handy material is usually made from organic fabrics such as cotton or old denim jeans, but you can also use other materials such as cotton balls and tampons. You can even substitute natural materials like dried moss, leaves, certain fungi, punk wood (spongy, rotting wood on the outside of a dead tree) and broken down or processed barks like willow or poplar. The process of making char cloth involves the material undergoing pyrolysis, which is the thermochemical decomposition of organic material at elevated temperatures in the absence of oxygen.

To make char cloth, you'll need to have a fire already going. An Altoids tin works great

for this process—since it has a hinged lid, you don't have to poke a hole in the top to let the gasses escape as you would for an airtight container. Once you have filled the metal container with your chosen material, place it into the fire and leave it there until you no longer see gasses or smoke escaping from the hinge or the hole you made. Once the smoke is gone, which should take approximately 10 to 15 minutes depending on how much you're making, remove the container from the fire, set it aside and let it cool. Do not open the container while hot because the charred material can ignite and render your char material useless. Char cloth will burn with the slightest spark and provides a slow-burning ember you can then transfer into your tinder bundle and blow into flame.

FLINT AND STEEL

Combined with char cloth or other charred material, you can easily make a fire from the spark created by flint and steel. A flint and steel set typically comes in a small tin box (convenient for making char cloth!) and features a high-carbon steel striker (usually in the shape of a D or C) and a piece of flint or chert.

To start a fire with flint and steel, begin by holding the striker in one hand with two or three fingers. In the other hand, hold the flint (or another rock) at a 45-degree angle with a piece of char cloth underneath.

Slam the striker against the edge of the rock to create hot sparks (this method is the precursor to the ferro rod, and you can see why).

You're scraping off small chunks of metal from the high carbon steel and causing oxidation, which is what makes the metal fragments ignite.

When the sparks hit the char cloth, it creates an ember. Place the ember inside your tinder, give it oxygen and bring it to flame.

PENCIL SHARPENER

While it can't be used to start a fire, this tool can help you prep your tinder and kindling. If you're planning to keep your kindling burning with fatwood (pg. 176), a pencil sharpener will make this material easier to use.

Break or cut off a small stick of fatwood and insert it into the pencil sharpener as you would a pencil. As you turn the stick, the sharpener will make paper-thin shavings. While the 90-degree spine on your knife can also be used to make flammable wood shavings, that method will make very fine powdery shavings. The pencil sharpener, however,

makes high-quality kindling and tinder.

FERRO ROD

As detailed on pg. 148, the ferro rod is one of the most efficient tools available when it comes to starting fires. Notice the one pictured here is orange—like the BIC lighter, you want to choose a bright color that can be easily spotted in case you drop it in the woods. There have been instances on survival reality TV shows in which contestants went home because they lost their ferro rod and were unable to start a friction fire due to the climate. As an additional precaution, it's a good idea to keep your rod on a lanyard to keep it from falling off your belt or out of your pocket.

> **Most ferro rods allow you to start more than 20,000 fires over the course of their lifespan.**

MAGNIFICATION LENS

When venturing out, it's always wise to have a way to start a fire with the sun's rays. Not only is a magnification lens effective, it also does not waste any resources. Plus, it has multiple purposes—you can use it to find and remove a splinter, for example.

Magnification lenses come in various shapes and sizes, so you'll want to choose one that's practical for your needs. The one pictured here is on a necklace to prevent it from being lost, like other items in this kit.

MAGNIFICATION MIRROR

Like the magnification lens, the magnification mirror serves multiple purposes. You can use it to start a fire on a sunny day, but you can also use it for signaling if you're lost. Or, use it as a mirror if you need to get something out of your eye or have the urge to shave while in the woods.

This particular mirror is a 10x magnifying mirror, which can typically be found in the cosmetics aisle at a local department store. To use it to start a fire, see pg. 177.

ADDITIONAL TOOLS

While these items are not essential to your fire kit, it never hurts to have additional resources available to keep the flames coming.

BAMBOO FIRE SAW

WHEN I FIRST saw the bamboo fire saw in a survival book, it blew my mind that you could start a fire by rubbing bamboo sticks together. After watching some videos online and seeing it in action, I did what any south Mississippi redneck would do: I drove around until I found bamboo!

Contrary to popular belief, hundreds of species of bamboo and cane grow in the eastern United States, especially in the Deep South. In Mississippi, I can drive about 5 miles and find five patches of bamboo; it grows everywhere. I have been camping in the middle of a national forest and found a patch of bamboo. Now, I'm not talking about the colossal, thick bamboo used to build various structures in Asia, but rather bamboo that grows up to about 1½ to 2 inches in diameter.

The great thing about bamboo is that everything you need to start your fire is included in the plant itself.

Step 1 First, select a dead stalk and cut a piece of bamboo roughly 18 to 24 inches long. When choosing your bamboo, look for a relatively straight piece that has dried out. Live bamboo is naturally green, and once it dies and dries, it turns yellowish. This method will not work with green bamboo.

Step 2 Take the 90-degree spine of your knife and scrape down the entire length of your piece of bamboo to create small shavings resembling strips of paper (bamboo fabric is made by refining shavings like these). Continue scraping until you have a pile of shavings that fills both of your hands cupped together. These shavings will be the base of your fire tinder, but you will also need some other type of tinder to place this in when you blow it into flame.

Step 3 Stand your bamboo stalk up and use your knife to baton through the stalk to split it in half. You can use another stick as a mallet to beat your knife down, but it should not be tough to separate the bamboo stalk. Once you have two pieces of bamboo, pick one to serve as the saw portion of your bamboo fire saw (it doesn't matter which you pick). Then, take your knife and shave one edge of the bamboo to the thickness of a butter knife blade. This portion will fit inside a groove and cause friction for the saw.

Step 4 Use your knife to drill a small hole in the center of and through the other piece of bamboo inside the stalk.

Step 5 Once you've made the hole, make a small cut where the hole is, perpendicular to the edge of the board. Do not cut all the way through the bamboo. You're only trying to make a groove for the saw to rest.

Step 6 Take your saw portion and rest one end against a tree while resting the other end on your hip (you can also

With bamboo, you can
sometimes get lucky and
find a very straight piece.

lean over the saw and put one end on the ground and the other on your chest, but this is not as comfortable). Take the tinder you scraped off your bamboo and place it over the hole inside your second bamboo stalk. You can use a tiny piece of bamboo to hold the tinder down so as not to burn your thumbs.

Step 7 Now that your tinder is in place, take the second bamboo stalk and rest the groove on the butter knife-thick piece of bamboo. Slowly start moving the top stalk back and forth. This is called seating the groove; you want to gradually add pressure and speed. Once you smell smoke, the track or groove will start looking black or burnt. Don't stop; let the dust accumulate and heat up, turning into ember. Keep going until you have plenty of smoke coming out (and you should still see smoke when you stop). Flip the board over and empty it into your other tinder bundle, then fold the bundle and blow it to flame.

It may take you a couple of tries before you start your first fire with a bamboo saw. You will be exhausted. Still, the satisfaction of starting a fire with a piece of bamboo is exhilarating, and you'll have a tremendous sense of accomplishment.

Drill slowly to avoid stabbing the whole blade straight through .

The groove should be just enough for the saw to rest.

You may be a bit winded by the time you blow the tinder to flame.

QUICK TIP

Bamboo can also be used to make anything from water storage containers to shelter materials to bowls, plates and cups.

FIRE WICK

THE FIRE WICK will not solve all your fire-related problems in the great outdoors; it's more of a handy little device you can use around camp. While it's more of a novelty item, the fire wick does have a lot going for it: It's practically windproof and water-resistant, it doesn't take long to make and it's very lightweight and easily packable.

Making a fire wick is also a fun project if you have kids, as it will get them involved in the great outdoors with a very hands-on introduction to starting fires. The applications for this item are endless, from burning a BBQ pit to starting a fire at the campsite in the middle of nowhere.

You will need:
- Petroleum jelly
- A small pot
- A burner such as a hot plate or camp stove
- A length of natural rope (manila, jute, sisal, hemp, cotton, etc.)
- A disposable fork
- Wax (I recommend tea light candles)
- 6-inch copper or PVC pipe, inner diameter equal to rope
- A disposable plate or paper towels
- A ferro rod

Be sure your rope has enough length to extend out of the pipe.

Step 1 Place the petroleum jelly in the pot and heat it until it liquefies, using enough jelly so that the liquid will cover the entire rope.

Step 2 Curl the rope up and use the plastic fork to place it in the liquefied jelly. Ensure the rope is completely covered so that the jelly can soak into all the fibers. Soak the rope until all bubbles disappear.

Step 3 Pour the petroleum jelly into another container and dispose of it or set it aside for another project. Place your wax into the pot to melt, ensuring you have enough to cover the rope completely. Soak the rope until all bubbles disappear.

Step 4 Remove the rope and place it on a disposable plate or paper towel to dry.

QUICK TIP

The fire wick can also be used around the house to light things such as a gas grill, charcoal grill or fish burner.

Ensure you can pull the rope in and out of the pipe without it getting stuck.

Once the wax is firm, insert the rope into the pipe.

Step 5 Before igniting the fire wick, fluff up the rope's end: Ensure all the fibers are exposed by rubbing it on a hard surface such as a log or breaking it up with your fingers.

Step 6 Use a ferro rod to ignite the rope. The petroleum jelly acts as an accelerant while the wax slows the burn and allows the rope to burn for a long time. To snuff it out, pull the rope into the pipe.

HOMEMADE FIRE BISCUITS

THERE ARE COUNTLESS variations of waterproof fire starters out there, but I make my own, which I call fire biscuits. A fire biscuit is very easy to make with just a few items you may already have around the house.

You will need:
- 1 package of cotton rounds or cotton balls (or dryer lint)
- 2 cups or bowls
- Charcoal lighter fluid
- Wax (Gulf Wax, candles, old crayons)
- Aluminum foil
- A disposable spoon

Step 1 Place several cotton rounds in a cup or bowl (I use an old wax pot, not pictured).

Step 2 Supersaturate the rounds with lighter fluid. They should be dripping wet.

Step 3 Melt wax in another cup or bowl.

Step 4 Lay out a strip of aluminum foil on your workspace. Place the wet cotton rounds on the foil.

Step 5 Use the disposable spoon to drip three spoonfuls of hot wax onto each cotton round.

Step 6 After the wax dries, flip the cotton rounds over and repeat Step 5 on the other side.

Step 7 Let the wax harden, then store the finished fire biscuits in a Ziploc bag.

QUICK TIP

You can use petroleum jelly instead of lighter fluid—just melt it down the same way as the wax.

Five Hacks for
FAST FIRES

If you have any of these resources available, you can get a roaring campfire going in no time.

1 THE FATWOOD METHOD

Fatwood goes by many names: lighter knot, pitch lighter, fat lighter, pitch wood and many more. Fatwood is great for fire because, once a coniferous tree dies, the sap collects in the dead tree or branch and the wood becomes rich in flammable terpene, a volatile hydrocarbon. This terpene evaporates, making the sap extremely hard and leaving you with very flammable wood.

There are roughly 125 different species of coniferous (or pine) trees worldwide. So the chances of you finding fatwood in your location are very high. Fatwood has a very intense turpentine smell (which smells similar to Pine-Sol) and once you've smelled it, you'll never forget that odor. Depending on the amount of sap collected, the wood's color ranges from yellow to dark gold.

When you find a dead pine tree or limb, take your knife and scrape the bark away to observe the color and smell. The bark pictured here was scraped away and shavings were made using the 90-degree spine of a knife. Use your ferro rod to generate a spark in the fatwood—it should erupt into flame, even if it is wet or damp. I once camped in the rain for six days and it rained so hard that the only way to keep the fire lit was with fatwood!

2 THE CATTAIL FLUFF METHOD

In addition to being a decent food option in a pinch, cattails can be used as tinder. The part at the top of the plant that looks like a sausage

3 THE MAGNIFYING GLASS METHOD

When I was a little boy, my brother and I would sit out in the woods and start fire after fire with the big 10x magnification glass our mom gave us. If she only knew half of the things we set on fire, we would have been in so much trouble. Creating fire with a magnification mirror or lens is a great option when supplies are limited because you're not using or expending any fuel—you just need the sun's rays.

Get your tinder bundle ready and place a piece of char cloth in the middle. If you're using a magnification mirror, hold your tinder bundle up and direct the sun's rays toward the bundle from the bottom. If you're using a magnification lens, hold the lens between the tinder and the sun. Now all you have to do is amplify the rays onto the char cloth until you get smoke or see the ember (which shouldn't take long at all).

Once you see the ember, fold the tinder bundle over the char cloth and slowly blow (as seen on pg. 159) until

(called the flower head) is made of thousands of seeds with fluff. This fluff resembles what you'd see on a dandelion or the down from a pillow and you can use it as tinder (more specifically "flash tinder," which means once a spark hits, it will ignite very quickly, almost like gasoline).

With the trickiness of this tinder in mind, you'll want another tinder source available when starting your fire. Place the cattail fluff on top of the other tinder source to increase your chance of getting steady flames going. It may take a few tries, but it can absolutely create a substantial fire.

you see a lot of smoke. As you see more smoke, continue to blow harder until you have flames straight from the sun's rays.

4 THE LIGHT BULB METHOD

I love being able to use a common item to create a fire in an emergency, and this method is no exception. Starting a fire with a glass light bulb is similar to methods that involve magnifying or concentrating the sun's rays onto fire tinder and char cloth or a char wick (pictured on right page, a char wick acts the same as char cloth and can also be used to wick water in a pinch). You must use a glass light bulb—you cannot use an LED or a plastic bulb.

First, carefully break the aluminum end off the bulb without damaging the bulb and pull out the guts. Rinse out the white powder used to make light softer, then fill the light bulb with clear water.

Get a bundle of tinder and char cloth or wick ready (don't get it wet). Magnify the sun until the light bulb gets hot.

Using your finger, find the hottest point. Careful not to burn yourself. Hold your char cloth, wick or tinder in that place and let the sun do its job. Focus the beam onto your tinder. You should soon see smoke, then all you have to do is transfer the char cloth or wick to your tinder and blow it into flame.

5 THE WATER BOTTLE METHOD

Fire and water are commonly thought of as opposites, but you can use a water bottle to make a fire if you know what you're doing. Certain round plastic water bottles amplify the sun's rays. In my experience, the best brand of bottled water to use for this fire-starting method is SmartWater, likely due to the bottle's distinct shape.

Fill the bottle with clear water and angle it so the sun is shining through the curve of the bottle. This will produce the exact same effect as a magnification lens or the light bulb filled with water. Concentrate the sun's beams onto the char cloth or tinder. Once you see smoke, you should be able to blow it into flame.

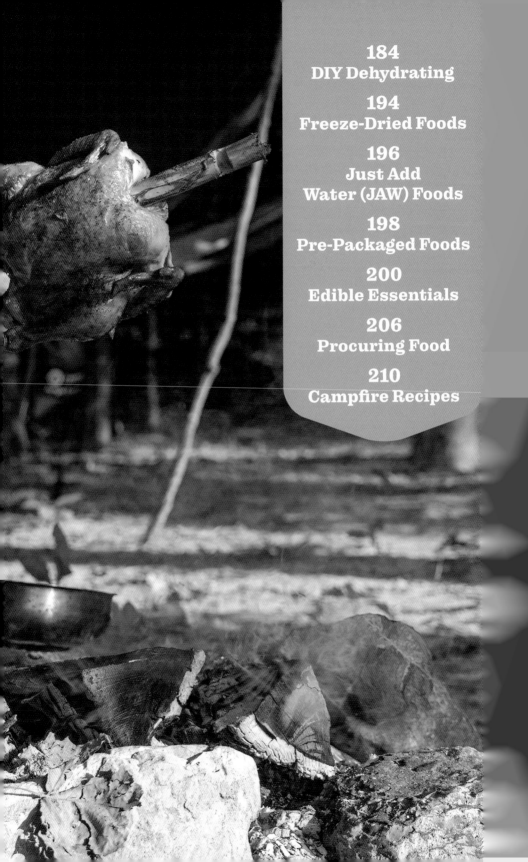

We all have our go-to foods when we're in the comfort of our own homes, but when heading out into the wilderness, a little outside-the-box (or in my case, potato chip bag) thinking is sometimes required. There are many things you can do to prepare before you go, even if you're planning to procure all your food while camping. For example, you can bring items such as flavor packets and seasoning to augment or enhance what you already have. No need to eat flavorless foods just because you're roughing it.

When you're planning to travel several miles into the wild, food becomes a major consideration for two main reasons: Food is heavy, but you need it to survive. Calories equal energy. During my time in the military, I ate more MREs (Meals Ready to Eat) than I can count. Sometimes they were good, sometimes they were horrible, but the fact is each one provided more than 2,000 calories. When you're in a situation where you're expending a lot of calories, you have to be able to replenish them. Activities such as rock climbing, hiking over hills, swimming or canoeing all require you to expend energy, and if you're not replacing those calories, you're going to get exhausted in no time. Trust me, your energy levels will get used up very quickly when primitive camping. But instead of explaining why you need food (which you likely already know), let's explore how to ensure you have enough when you need it.

Dehydrated eggs and canned meats provide a quick cure for hunger.

it under a vacuum to remove the moisture. The major advantage of freeze-dried food over dehydrated food is its drastically reduced weight. An 8-pound roast that has been cooked and freeze-dried will weigh less than a pound, whereas the same 8-pound roast turned into jerky will weigh 3 pounds. When reconstituted, freeze-dried food retains the same texture as freshly cooked food. The downside to freeze-drying is that it is costly. Even a small freeze-drying unit can be cost-prohibitive for many people. In comparison, a commercial dehydrator can cost you somewhere in the neighborhood of $400, but you can also find small models for as low as $20.

JUST ADD WATER FOOD

Readily available at pretty much any grocery store, Just Add Water (JAW) food is what it sounds like. Mashed potatoes, broccoli and rice, and macaroni and cheese are just a few examples. All you need is access to water and you'll have a meaningful meal in no time.

PRE-PACKAGED FOOD

Popular pre-packaged foods for primitive camping include sardines, cans of beans and Vienna sausages, to name a few. These can add a lot of variety and flavor to the meals you make in the woods.

PROCURED FOOD

Procured food is anything gained from hunting, fishing or foraging that augments what you have brought with you. These require some additional skills and knowledge, of course, but the results are well worth the effort.

For our purposes, food can be broken down into five categories: dehydrated, freeze-dried, Just Add Water (JAW), pre-packaged and procured.

DEHYDRATED FOOD

A dehydrator removes all the moisture from food items by applying low heat over a period of time. This is the same principle as cutting venison into small, thin strips and hanging it out to dry in the sun, just on a smaller scale and in a controlled environment. Dehydrating your food will often make it hard and brittle, depending on the food.

FREEZE-DRIED FOOD

Freeze-dried food is different from dehydrated food in that it involves freezing the food and then thawing

DIY DEHYDRATING

DEHYDRATING YOUR FOOD is a fairly simple process and there are several different kinds of dehydrators you can use. Small, cheap dehydrators can be found at a department store, while bigger ones that are more in line with commercial dehydrators can be purchased from the likes of Bass Pro Shops, Cabela's or a similar store. The dehydrator I use is in between the consumer and commercial brands and is relatively large; it has five trays, a temperature dial and a timer to dehydrate the food for a specific duration. You can dehydrate pretty much anything, but one of the first things many people want to make when they start dabbling in dehydrating food is beef jerky.

BEEF JERKY

Beef jerky is extremely versatile; you can eat it on its own or add it to beans, stews or soups for a more complete meal. I've been making beef jerky for more than 30 years now and have experimented with hundreds of different flavors and many recipes— I've yet to find a beef jerky recipe I haven't liked.

To make your own beef jerky, obtain a beef roast from your local grocery's meat department. You can have them slice it up for you, or you can slice it yourself (I prefer the former to save time). Jerky should be cut into sandwich slices (less than one-eighth of an inch) for faster dehydrating and best results. The perfect piece of meat for a jerky is the eye of round roast, but any roast will work. This particular cut is usually not very expensive and has less fat on it. If you want your jerky to have maximum shelf-life, cut the fat off the roast before dehydrating it as the oils in the fat will cause the meat to go bad within a few days. If you only plan on using the jerky in a stew or beans, removing the fat isn't essential, but you should use the jerky within a few days of making it.

Flavoring your jerky is simple; just use your favorite store-bought marinade. I often use Moore's Original Marinade, which I like because it has a lot of flavor but not a lot of salt. I sometimes season my jerky with nothing more than hot sauce and creole seasoning, and once all my friends and family tried it, they begged for more.

Step 1 Place the sliced meat in a large bowl, then pour on some marinade. Toss the meat until all the slices appear evenly coated in the marinade. Continue to toss about every 10-15 minutes until the meat changes to a color that matches the marinade, then let it sit and marinate in the bowl for about an hour.

Step 2 Place your meat on the dehydrator racks without much overlap. Overlapping slices will stick together and take longer to dehydrate.

QUICK TIP
You can rehydrate beef jerky by soaking it in a sauce, broth or other liquid and letting it sit for several hours in a sealed environment.

Step 3 Once you have layered your rack, sprinkle desired seasoning such as salt, herbs and spices all over the jerky to give it more flavor.

Step 4 Place your racks of meat in the dehydrator.

Step 5 If your dehydrator has a thermostat, set it to 145-150 degrees F for 5 hours. Once the time is up, check it to see if the jerky has reached the consistency you like. If you want dryer, crispier jerky, add more time. Once the consistency is to your liking, remove the jerky and let it cool to room temperature.

Step 6 You are now ready to either vacuum seal the jerky with a food saver, which will allow it to stay fresh for months, or use a zipper-lock bag to keep it fresh for the duration of your trip.

EGGS

There's nothing like scrambled eggs cooked on an open fire, but taking whole eggs with you on a camping trip isn't exactly feasible. While small packable egg carriers are easy to find, you risk cracking the eggs, and the added weight is not conducive to hiking. Fortunately, you can make powdered eggs for your trip in just a few easy steps.

NOTE: If you dehydrate whole eggs, you have to separate the yolks from the whites and dehydrate them separately. For this reason, it's easier to buy a few cartons of egg whites.

Step 1 Line the tray of your dehydrator with parchment paper. You can buy parchment paper made specifically for different dehydrators. The center

Most liquid egg whites come in containers that allow easy pouring.

of the dehydrator is where the airflow comes through, so if using standard parchment paper, you will have to cut a hole in the middle to allow the air to circulate. Pour the egg whites onto the paper-lined tray. Repeat the process until you either run out of eggs or trays. Place the trays in the dehydrator and let them dry at 140 degrees F for 10 hours or until completely dry (you will know they're dry because they will turn completely yellow).

Step 2 Place the egg whites in a blender and pulverize them into fine powder. The same result can also be achieved by placing the eggs in a zipper-lock bag and pulverizing them

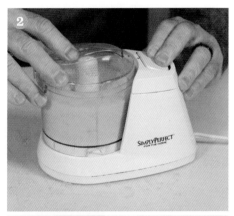

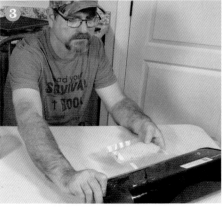

with a rolling pin.

Step 3 Once the eggs have turned into fine powder, store them in a vacuum-sealed or zipper-lock bag. When kept in a vacuum-sealed bag in a cool, dry environment, they can last 5-10 years.

Step 4 To reconstitute the eggs when ready to eat, mix 1 tablespoon egg powder with three tablespoons water. Stir a few times and let sit until the eggs have been reconstituted, then cook as you would a regular egg.

TOMATOES

Tomatoes make a fantastic, healthy snack and are so flavorful. For dehydrating, you want ripe tomatoes; you don't want them to be overripe but they also shouldn't be underripe or green. You do not have to cut the stems or the butts off the tomatoes for this process. Many distributors use a thin layer of edible wax on their produce to make them look more appealing in the store, so be sure to rinse your tomatoes under warm water to get rid of that wax as well as any dirt.

Step 1 Starting at the butt end, slice the tomato about an eighth inch thick. Repeat as needed depending on the number of tomatoes and/or dehydrator trays.

Step 2 Line the dehydrator racks with parchment paper and place the sliced tomatoes on the racks. Set the temperature to 145-150 degrees F for

> ### QUICK TIP
> **Don't worry about overdoing it—the longer you dehydrate something, the crispier it will become.**

When slicing, be sure to hold zucchini firmly to keep it from rolling.

Be sure to completely peel the onions—it's easy to miss a layer.

5-7 hours (you may have to go a little longer depending on the thickness of the slices).

Step 3 When finished, you should have very crispy, delicious tomato chips, which can be eaten as is or crushed up added to other foods for flavor when camping. I often eat all my tomato chips before I get the chance to cook with them.

SQUASH AND ZUCCHINI

Making chips from dehydrated squash and zucchini is a fantastic, healthy alternative to potato chips. They give you the same crunch as a potato chip, and you can add them to a pot of stew. I have never been a huge fan of cooked squash, but I will eat these all day long.

Step 1 Cut your yellow squash or zucchini into slices approximately a quarter inch thick. If you do not cut them thick enough, the center of the chip will disintegrate in the dehydrator, leaving you just the skin of the vegetable. Place on a dehydrator tray and lightly sprinkle with salt and pepper.

Step 2 Dehydrate at 145-150 degrees F for 7–10 hours (thicker slices might take a little longer).

Step 3 Once finished, let cool to room temperature, then store in a zipper-lock or vacuum-sealed bag.

ONIONS

Onions are a big cooking staple. So many commercial seasonings start with onion powder and salt as a base. Dehydrating your onions will leave all the nutrients intact and prepare them for nearly any cooking need. Once

QUICK TIP

Any onion will work for this process—I tend to use yellow onions because they're nearly always cheaper.

dehydrated, you can crush them into a powder and sprinkle them onto food as you're cooking, or you can throw them into the pot to be cooked or rehydrated. **NOTE:** This process will make your house smell like an enormous onion! Make sure you do it in a well-ventilated area.

Step 1 Remove all the skin and cut the onion in half, then slice about a quarter inch thick.

Step 2 Place the onions on the racks and set the dehydrator to 145-150 degrees F for 7-10 hours. This will ensure they get nice and crispy. Add more time if all the onions are not completely dehydrated.

Step 3 Remove the onions and cool to room temperature. Store in a zipper-lock

or vacuum-sealed bag. You can crush the onions into a powder before storage or keep them as whole flakes. This is the same process used for onion flakes and other onion products found in the seasoning aisle at a grocery store.

MUSHROOMS

Dehydrated mushrooms can be reconstituted whole while cooking, pulverized into a powder to make gravy or just used to add flavoring to your camping food. It's often particularly easy to dry mushrooms because most of them are pre-packaged, pre-sliced and all you have to do is place them on the dehydrator racks.

Step 1 If using whole mushrooms, wash and slice a quarter inch

Buying sliced mushrooms will save time, but you'll have to dehydrate sooner as they don't last as long as whole mushrooms.

thick. You don't have to put them on parchment paper, but if your dehydrator racks have larger openings, some may fall through in the drying process.

Step 2 Place the mushrooms on the drying racks and set the dehydrator at 150 degrees F for five to seven hours. Once dried, they should feel like styrofoam and snap with a crisp sound when you bend them. If they do not snap, dry for a few more hours. Once dehydrated, store them in a zipper-lock bag or vacuum seal them.

MUSHROOM SHRINKAGE

Mushrooms are my absolute favorite item to dehydrate and use in my food. But be warned: Mushrooms shrink a lot during this process! If you were to dehydrate 3 pounds of mushrooms, for example, they will only weigh about 1 ounce once dried—which is great when you want to pack light but have quite the appetite.

Mushrooms pair well with small game meals such as frog legs.

Green peppers will usually be the cheapest bell pepper option.

BELL PEPPERS

Dehydrated bell peppers are a flavorful addition to beans or stews when camping. However, bell peppers shrink even more than mushrooms do; five bell peppers will take up two entire racks in my dehydrator, but once dried, they will only fill three-quarters of a cup and barely weigh more than 1 ounce.

Step 1 Halve and deseed peppers.
Step 2 Slice peppers a quarter inch thick and place them on dehydrator racks. Dry at 145-150 degrees F for 7-10 hours. They're done when they're shriveled and very brittle to the touch.

QUICK TIP
Dehydrated vegetables can be stored in a vacuum-sealed bag for up to two years.

GET CREATIVE

The options are endless when it comes to dehydrating vegetables. You can even dehydrate canned foods such as diced tomatoes, tomato paste, mushrooms, asparagus and many others via the same process you would use for fresh produce. It's rewarding and even entertaining when you find new foods to dehydrate and use in different meals. I routinely purchase discounted vegetables, cut the bad spots off and dehydrate them. I usually vacuum-seal them and throw them into the freezer, where they last for about two years (but I always use them well before that).

Step 3 Store in a zipper-lock bag.
NOTE: Do not store in a vacuum seal bag unless turning into a powder—dehydrated peppers can have sharp points that may puncture the bag.

Dehydrating is great for saving extra produce that would have gone to waste.

FREEZE-DRIED FOOD

FREEZE-DRIED FOOD IS EASY to make and convenient to carry, from scrambled eggs with biscuits to beef stroganoff to hearty chili. Unlike many other quick and simple camping food options, freeze-dried foods are usually an entire meal that can feed one person or more if needed. Making pre-packaged, freeze-dried camping meals is a slightly expensive endeavor upfront, but many folks find the benefits to be well worth the price.

Collecting many freeze-dried foods upfront will help you eliminate food concerns for future trips.

ENDLESS OPTIONS

With all the containers pictured here, you could make 40-50 campsite meals—all you need is a zipper-lock bag and an imagination. Any freeze-dried product should have the conversion tables printed on the container so you know how much

to use as if it were fresh food. For example, I love chicken and rice, so I would combine ¼ cup freeze-dried chicken with ¼ cup freeze-dried green peas and ½ cup instant rice. Throw in a chicken bouillon cube or two (or add ½ tablespoons bouillon powder), add the recommended amount of water and you have a fantastic meal for two, ready to heat up when you're in the woods.

THE COST OF CONVENIENCE

A small freeze dryer can cost between $3,000 and $5,000, which is why freeze-dried foods are off the table for many campers. Plus, the foods themselves can often cause sticker shock—one large can of beef can cost between $75 and $100. The benefit, though, is that it's a large can that will go a lot further than a $10 complete meal. If you invest in a few cans of various meats and vegetables, you can save money in the long run by eliminating the need to purchase individual meals, and you have the added benefit of knowing exactly what ingredients you're adding to your food. The shelf life of an unopened container can be up to 25 years, and if you vacuum seal the opened contents with an oxygen absorber, they should store for the same amount of time. A well-stored open can will still last you up to a year.

You won't break the bank (or your back) carrying JAW foods into the woods.

JUST ADD WATER (JAW) FOODS

WITH JUST ADD Water (JAW) FOOD, the convenience is in the name. JAW foods are lightweight, easy-to-use pre-packaged meals found on the shelves of nearly every grocery or convenience store. When planning a camping trip, many people never consider bringing a pack of Knorr chicken-flavored rice and pasta, Jalapeño Cheddar Pasta Roni, Quaker instant oatmeal or Idahoan Baby Reds Mashed Potatoes (a personal favorite around my campsite). But these common items are perfect for the great outdoors—all you have to do is add the

them an appealing option if you're not ready to invest in the world of freeze-drying. Plus, they're incredibly lightweight, leaving plenty of room to pack additional snacks and items you may want for your trip.

HASH BROWNS

JAW hash browns are worth noting because they can be used for many purposes. Their most common use is as a breakfast staple, but you can also use them to make potato soup or add them to a dish to thicken it up or make it more calorie-dense (which is often necessary when you're constantly burning calories in the woods). These potatoes are boiled, grated, dehydrated and boxed. This process makes them very lightweight and easy to carry, and it also makes them very simple to make and eat.

contents to a pot of water, bring to a boil and stir.

Many of these make great main dishes on their own, but you can always add some variety of meat such as summer sausage, Spam or even beef jerky to make a more complete meal. JAW foods can often be found for about $1, sometimes less, making

PRE-PACKAGED FOODS have their pros and cons. The pros: They're tasty, include staples you're already used to eating, and are convenient to obtain and cost-effective. The cons: The packaging makes them bulky to carry, and the food itself generally adds a considerable amount of weight to your pack. Since we want to minimize how much we carry when heading out, pre-packaged foods may not seem like the wisest choice—but fortunately, there are plenty of options on the market that meet primitive camping standards.

Tortillas, Vienna sausages, Beanee Weenee and smoked fish steaks are just a few of the pre-packaged food items you can rely on. Energy and protein bars pack plenty of calories into their small size, and tuna, while typically sold in less-than-ideal cans, can also be found in small, lightweight packets perfect for camping. A few tuna packets can be used for lunches over the course of a few days, and each adds only a few ounces to your backpack.

SUMMER SAUSAGE

Summer sausage is an excellent pre-packaged food that does not need to be refrigerated before opening. I often eat summer sausage for breakfast with eggs, and I also like to add it to beans for a more complete meal. Once opened,

CANNED MEAT CONSIDERATIONS

Sardines, Spam, Vienna sausage and other canned meats may be appealing for various reasons, but the major downside to these items is that they weigh a lot. Depending on how far you're trekking through the woods, a can of Spam may not seem like something that would slow you down that much. But if you're hiking 10 miles into the backcountry, for example, that one can will seriously start to weigh you down. The other downside to canned meats is that they need to be eaten immediately once opened because they start to spoil quickly.

summer sausage keeps for several days. You can eat it right out of the package or mix it into anything from mac and cheese to rice to soups and stews. It also makes meal planning easy: Purchase two or three small summer sausages and use one for beans, one for breakfast, etc. I always bring summer sausage when I venture out—it's almost as essential as my flashlight!

TORTILLAS

Before heading out, I always do some pre-packaging of my own by placing several small tortillas in a vacuum seal bag. You can purchase a 40-pack of tortillas from a wholesale club and divide them as necessary—they last a very long time once vacuum-sealed. Tortillas can be used for breakfast, lunch, dinner or any time you need some form of bread to boost your calorie count.

Summer sausage doesn't need to be cooked but tastes even better when it is (especially over a campfire).

THESE VERSATILE ITEMS are great for any primitive camper looking to make a variety of meals in the woods, and they also won't weigh you down.

DRIED BEANS

Dried beans are usually sold by the pound, which makes them perfect for the primitive camper calculating the weight of their backpack. Plus, a little goes a long way: One pound of beans can give you two high-quality meals with the addition of summer sausage and instant rice. Beans are a fantastic food source for camping because they are a complex carbohydrate that takes longer to break down than simple carbs like sugar. And since they take longer to digest, they keep you feeling full longer.

It's wise to purchase a large bag (4 pounds or so) of dried beans and divide it up into zipper-lock bags. For guidance, use this list of common conversions from *The Spruce Eats* (a handy website with recipes and measurements for dry goods) for weights and yields:

1 pound dried beans = about 6 cups cooked beans

1 part dried beans = 3 parts cooked beans

1 cup dried beans = 3 cups cooked beans

⅓ cup dried beans = 1 cup cooked beans

I prefer dried red kidney beans, or simply "red beans," as we call them in the South. They don't take very long to cook and are very flavorful.

Soaking beans tends to cut down on the cooking time: I place a half pound of beans in a pot and cover them with water in the morning, and when I return to camp that evening, they are softened and will cook quickly. In addition to making them easier to cook, soaking your beans makes them a little easier to digest. To wit,

my grandmother Grace would call this process "soaking the fart out of the beans." Your fellow campers will thank you.

INSTANT RICE
Instant rice is approximately half the weight of regular parboiled rice, making it a valuable asset when heading to the great outdoors. Brands such as Minute Rice and Uncle Ben's are known for their spin on this convenient starchy grain. Instant rice takes very little time to cook (hence the name) because you simply rehydrate it in boiling water. This item goes a long way when paired with any meat or fish you're cooking and can also be used in beans and soups.

LIPTON ONION SOUP MIX
This stuff is a gold mine when you're

Dried beans can provide you plenty of protein If you're low on meat and eggs during a trip.

Red kidney Beans

camping. Not only can it be used to season anything you catch in the wild from fish to armadillos, it can also be used as originally intended: to make soup. Add some other items you've packed or foraged along the way and soon you'll have a calorie-dense nutritious dinner. A couple pouches of Lipton onion soup mix can always be found in my food bag when I venture into the woods.

PEANUT BUTTER

I remember a camping trip with my brother where, over the course of six days, we couldn't catch a fish to save our lives (which is how it goes sometimes). We were running out of food and feeling extremely weak and tired. Eventually, I remembered I brought a small jar of peanut butter with me, and I opened it up and went to town! I felt rejuvenated in just a few minutes from eating this often-overlooked item.

Peanut butter is a fantastic camping food because it's rich in protein, minerals and vitamins and also high in calories. When you're fatigued from hiking and the general physical toll of camping, peanut butter can restore your energy. The beautiful thing about peanut butter is that it can also be found in powder form, which is, of course, much lighter. The powdered version has fewer vitamins, minerals and fats than regular peanut butter but it will still provide you with energy. Peanut butter also comes in squeeze packets, another handy alternative for primitive campers.

Once opened, peanut butter has a shelf life of about two to three months.

Drinking black coffee will help lighten your load even more.

DRINK PACKETS

Drink packets are lightweight solutions for flavoring river or lake water. For instance, if you didn't filter your water and decided to boil it and drink it, it would still taste like lake water. This is where a strawberry lemonade drink packet comes in handy. It will flavor your water and, at the same time, keep you from craving something else (such as fruit juice or soda) for extended periods when camping.

GREEN TEA

By bringing a few green tea bags on a trip, you can boost your immune system and also give yourself a nice little treat to look forward to. If you're used to drinking caffeine every day and then head to the woods without any, you will get a headache from caffeine withdrawal. Green tea will help prevent that.

INSTANT COFFEE

Some people will object to this strategy, but it's worth mentioning. While you may have seen cinematic adventure videos in which people find the perfect camping spot and brew coffee, the cup of joe I prefer when camping is a bit different. Instant coffee packets are sold in mass quantities and are incredibly convenient to carry in the woods. Plus, they give you the morning boost you need to kickstart your day and can help eliminate caffeine withdrawal headaches. And of course, with these single-use packets, you won't have to worry about bulky coffee pots, filters and other brewing items, which can all be quite cumbersome to pack and carry.

POWDERED MILK

Powdered milk is great in coffee if you are used to having cream. If you plan to make biscuits in the woods (pg. 212), you can add a little powdered milk to the self-rising flour and egg powder for a slightly richer flavor. And if you're feeling ambitious in your campsite cooking endeavors, powdered milk can be used to make beef stroganoff.

SHORTENING

Shortening is any fat that becomes a solid at room temperature, such as margarine, bacon grease, tallow, lard or vegetable shortening. It's an excellent resource when camping—

QUICK TIP

The small bottles for shampoo and lotion found in the travel aisle of pharmacies work perfectly for storing and transporting seasonings and oil.

instead of hauling liquid oil into the woods, you can purchase shortening in blocks the size of butter sticks or a small tub. Shortening is great for frying fish, mouse, squirrel or any other critter you catch (I realize many people won't want to eat the likes of squirrels, mice or other rodents, but I like to!). It's also handy if you plan on baking in the backcountry.

You can lighten your load even more by combining certain seasonings.

Powdered milk is a lightweight, versatile item that makes many meals possible.

You don't need a nice
lure to catch fish, but it
doesn't hurt to bring one.

PROCURING FOOD

ONE OF THE most challenging ways to feed yourself in the great outdoors is by procuring food at or near the campsite. Fishing, hunting, trapping and foraging are categories of food procurement that can allow you to augment anything you bring. Supplementing your food with fish is a huge advantage not only for the nutritional value, but also because it can allow you to keep some of the food you brought as reserves if you stay for an extended trip. Hunting can also yield rations that will sustain you for a very long time. If it is legal in your location, setting snares can be very effective in obtaining rabbits and squirrels. However, if you're familiar with trapping or snaring small wild game, you know they have a limited amount of fat on them. You can eat a rabbit every day and still starve due to how lean the meat is. Rabbit meat does have protein, which you need, but it lacks sufficient fat to keep you healthy over an extended period. Maintaining certain fat levels in your diet helps maintain your brain function, keeping you thinking clearly.

Foraging (if you know what to look for) can significantly augment your meals. Ensure you know how to identify wild plants, berries or mushrooms before you consume them. There are many lookalikes that can make you extremely sick and even be deadly. When it comes to mushrooms, if you don't know exactly what kind you're looking at, don't touch it. The *National Audubon Society Field Guide to North American Mushrooms* can help you identify many species. There are hundreds of edible mushrooms but thousands of poisonous ones, and out of the hundreds of edible ones, many have a very toxic lookalike. When it comes to foraging wild plants for food, one of my favorite books to reference is *Edible Wild Plants* by Thomas S. Elias and Peter A. Dykeman. *Edible Wild Plants* demonstrates how to use each plant and the region, habitat and season in which it grows. Most importantly, it has numerous photographs of each edible plant so you can make a positive identification. In addition to books, many state universities have programs or workshops with botanists offering information on the edible plants in the area.

One of the most important aspects of procuring food from the environment

SNAKE SNACK

Snakes are an easy food to obtain. Most of the time, a snake can be found curled up in a defensive position ready to strike. Use a long stick with a fork to pin its head to the ground. At this point, you can dispatch it with your knife, but *make sure you maintain pressure on the head*. Once cleaned and cooked, be careful of the bones.

PINE NEEDLE TEA

There is only one type of pine-bearing tree in North America that is harmful to humans: the yew pine. Despite its name, it isn't technically a pine tree. The yew pine is mildly toxic and may cause nausea, vomiting and diarrhea when ingested. It can be identified by its small shrubs and sharp pointed needles that lack white lines underneath. All other pine or coniferous trees can be used to make tea with the tree's needles. Pine, fir, spruce and cedar can all be used to create an all-natural tea rich in vitamin C and antioxidants. This tea will boost your immune system, energize you and even soothe common cold symptoms (Virginia pine and white pine are particularly good for this). Plus, it tastes like the smell of Christmas.

Directions:
1. Collect a half-inch diameter of pine needles (pictured).
2. Boil a pot of water. While the water is boiling, cut the needles into thirds.
3. Remove the water from the fire and throw the needles into the pot. Cover and let stand for 15 minutes.
4. Once the needles turn lime green or yellowish, the tea is ready to drink.
5. Use a paper filter or place a handkerchief over your cup to filter out the needles as you pour.

is knowing how to get the most nutritional value out of it. During long-term camping, your body will start breaking down your fat reserves and using them for energy (I routinely lose 10 to 12 pounds if not more on an 8 to 10 day trip). To counter this, one of the best ways to get all the vitamins, minerals and fats from your food while camping is to boil everything and make a soup. Granted, you will get tired of eating soups, but you will ensure you retain all the fats and other nutrients that your body will need when expending lots of energy.

QUICK TIP
The parts of game animals that can't be eaten can often be repurposed. Entrails can be used as bait for fishing or trapping other animals.

Lion's mane mushrooms can be found on logs and living oak, maple and beech trees.

Oyster mushrooms grow on or near trees and are safe to eat after cooking.

Boiling your food ensures you get all the nutrients, such as fats you need for energy on extended trips.

Quick Campfire
RECIPES

**When hunger strikes after a long hike,
these easy meals will come in handy.**

Southern Red Beans

**This Southern staple tastes great no
matter where you are in the world.**

INGREDIENTS

1   lb dried red or kidney beans
    Dehydrated onion flakes to taste
    Dehydrated bell peppers to taste
    Salt and pepper or Creole
      seasoning to taste
½ lb summer sausage, cubed
    Powdered dehydrated
      mushrooms to taste
1   cup instant rice

DIRECTIONS

1. Place beans, onions and bell peppers
in a pot with water and let soak for 2-3
hours.
2. Add salt and pepper or Creole
seasoning and heat to a boil. Once
boiling, add summer sausage. Cover
and let simmer, stirring frequently.
3. Once the beans begin to soften, stir
in the mushrooms. The water should
begin to thicken slightly as you stir.
4. In a separate pot, bring 1 cup of
water to a boil. Add 1 cup instant rice,
remove from heat, cover and let sit
until all the water is absorbed. Serve
the beans over the rice.

Breakfast Skillet

**Prepare for a long day of hiking with
this simple, protein-packed meal.**

INGREDIENTS

6–8   Tbsp powdered eggs
18–24 Tbsp water to reconstitute
       the eggs
       Spam or summer sausage,
         diced, to taste
       Dehydrated tomato chips,
         crushed, to taste

DIRECTIONS

1. In a frying pan or skillet,
reconstitute dehydrated eggs.
2. Mix in Spam or summer sausage
and dehydrated tomato chips. Cook as
you would regular eggs and serve.

Biscuits

When I cook these biscuits on a trip, I'm reminded of John 6:35: "Then Jesus said, 'I am the bread of life. Whoever comes to me will never go hungry. And whoever believes in me will never be thirsty.'"

INGREDIENTS
- 2 cups self-rising flour
- 3 Tbsp powdered eggs
- ¼ cup powdered milk
- 1 cup water

DIRECTIONS
1. In a bowl, add flour, eggs, milk and 1 cup water. Mix all ingredients together and add more water as needed until you have a good dough.

2. Add flour to your hands to pick up the dough and divide into equal biscuits. Cook biscuits in a Dutch oven or similar pot until golden brown.

NOTE: Each fire is different, so check biscuits regularly to ensure they don't burn.

Chili Mac

This one takes a little work but is entirely worth it on a cool fall night in the woods. Although you can purchase chili mac freeze-dried and ready-to-eat, it tastes better when you make it from scratch.

INGREDIENTS
- 1 box mac and cheese
- 1 can bean-free chili, dehydrated and powdered
  Instant nonfat powdered milk (as needed according to mac and cheese box)

DIRECTIONS
1. Cook macaroni according to package directions. In a separate pot, add water to dehydrated chili and heat until it returns to pre-dehydrated consistency.

2. Once the macaroni is done cooking, continue following the directions. If making the powdered cheese kind, use instant nonfat powdered milk.

3. Add chili, stir well and serve.

QUICK TIP
Dehydrate the chili well before a trip and store it in the freezer until you head to the woods.

Dutch Oven Chicken

Chicken is delicious no matter how you cook it, but while camping, I especially love cooking a whole chicken in a Dutch oven.

INGREDIENTS

- 3 slices bacon
- 1 large onion, sliced
- 1 bell pepper, sliced
- 1 cup sliced mushrooms
  Baby red potatoes
- 1 whole small chicken or Cornish hen
  Flavored dry rub or seasoning (your favorite), to taste

DIRECTIONS

1. Place bacon in cast iron Dutch oven or skillet over fire. Once you have some fat rendered from the bacon, add all vegetables and stir to combine.

2. Add dry rub or seasoning and place the chicken in the middle of the Dutch oven with the veggies around it. Hang the pot on a tripod (pg. 238) or scrape some coals off the fire and place around the oven (pg. 226).

3. Let the chicken roast until the breast meat flakes off down to the bone with a fork. Chicken should be cooked to 170 degrees F.

QUICK TIP

If you wish to avoid the hormones typically found in store-bought whole chicken, the Cornish hen is a breed of chicken that can be substituted. Cornish hens weigh 1–2 pounds.

Energizing Vegetable Soup

As mentioned on pg. 201, using Lipton onion soup mix as a soup base is an excellent option when you need to cook up a source of energy.

INGREDIENTS

- Summer sausage or fish (fillet with no bones work best), to taste
- 1 packet Lipton onion soup mix
  Mixed dehydrated or fresh chopped vegetables, to taste

DIRECTIONS

1. Fill a pot with water as needed according to soup mix directions. If using summer sausage, cut into cubes and place in the pot. If using fresh-caught fish, place in pot and bring to a boil.

2. Add soup mix and vegetables to pot and boil until fish has fallen apart (summer sausage will not fall apart). Once dehydrated vegetables are reconstituted, or fresh veggies are soft, soup is ready. **NOTE:** Dehydrated vegetables can be used in place of fresh—simply add 1 cup of water with this step.

QUICK TIP

Beef jerky can be cooked and reconstituted as a meat substitute in any recipe. It takes a long time for jerky to become soft, but it's worth the wait if it's your only protein option.

COOKING

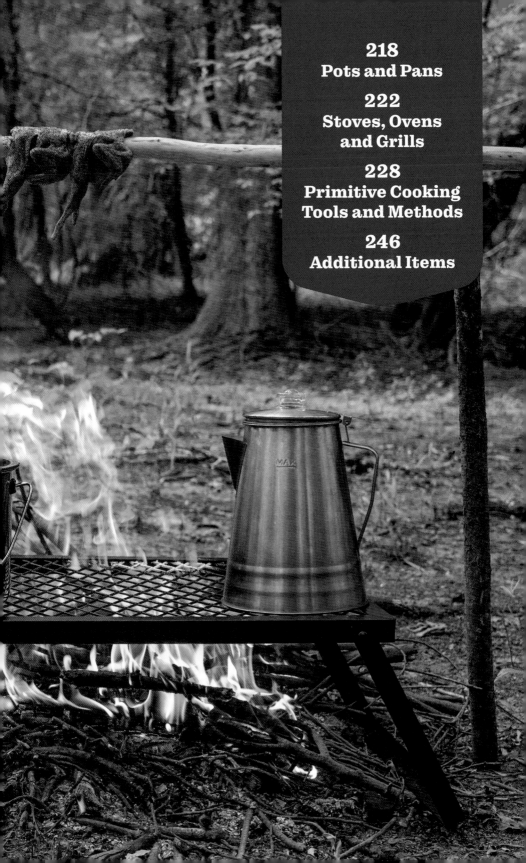

C ooking is one of my favorite things to do when I'm camping—it's a great way to hone skills, and it brings joy to the end of your day. This chapter will cover how to cook your food with various methods and also apply a little bushcraft to make a few "appliances." Once you learn the basics and start building the things that'll help you master the art of cooking in the great outdoors, you'll be well on your way to the end result: a full stomach!

The hardest part of cooking outdoors, whether frying or roasting, is ensuring your food is cooked to a safe temperature. Most campers will not have a food thermometer and will be left to do some guesswork. Luckily, when cooking the likes of poultry and beef, you can get a good indication of whether it's safe to eat by inserting your knife into the meat and observing the juices that run out. Generally, if the juices are clear and no blood is present, your food is safe to consume.

LOGS OR ROCKS
An effortless way to cook on an open fire is by using two logs of relatively

COOKING TEMPS
If you want to be extra cautious, pack a food thermometer. According to the USDA, the following foods should be cooked to the following internal temperatures:

Beef, pork, veal and lamb steaks, chops, roasts:
145 degrees F (62.8 degrees C)
Ground meats: 160 degrees F (71.1 degrees C)
Ground poultry: 165 degrees F (73.9 degrees C)
Ham, fresh or smoked (uncooked):
145 degrees F (62.8 degrees C)
Fully cooked ham: 165 degrees F (73.9 degrees C)
All poultry (breasts, whole bird, legs, thighs, wings, ground poultry, giblets and stuffing): 165 degrees F (73.9 degrees C)
Eggs: 160 degrees F (71.1 degrees C)
Fish and shellfish: 145 degrees F (62.8 degrees C)
Frogs and snakes: 145 degrees F (62.8 degrees C)

the same diameter spaced the width of your pot or pan. Scrape your coals into a pile, place your logs on each side, then set your pot or pan on the logs. Green wood tends to work best for this. This method has cooked more camp breakfasts for me than any other. You can feed the coals between the logs if more heat is needed. Rocks can be used similarly, but you will usually need three and it tends to be more difficult to find three rocks that are roughly the same size. This method will also reduce some weight in your backpack if you are hiking long distances, as you won't need to carry anything more than a pot or pan.

OPEN COALS

For quick cooking, you can rake coals to the side of your fire and place your pot or pan directly on the coals. This will begin to choke the coals but keep them hot enough to cook eggs and sausage. You can also nestle your water bottle directly against the edge of the coals to boil water for coffee. Open coals paired with a stainless steel or cast iron skillet is an easy way to cook fish or meat.

Beans and grilled pork chops make a classic campfire meal.

POTS AND PANS

AS DISCUSSED IN the Water and Gear sections, one of the most essential items you can carry into the woods is a metal container. As long as you choose the best type of metal for your needs, packing pots and pans for your camping trip will pay dividends in your campsite "kitchen."

TITANIUM

Titanium pots are incredibly lightweight and come in various sizes. Titanium is usually used for smaller cookware such as cups and lightweight pots and is ideal for boiling drinking water (pg. 60) and reconstituting freeze-dried foods. Cooking in titanium can quickly burn your food because the metal gets hotter in certain hot spots.

ALUMINUM

From cups to 24-quart pots (or bigger), aluminum is a lightweight option that has been a camper go-to for a long time. Aluminum tends to have fewer hot spots than titanium—depending on the pot's style and thickness, it cooks food more evenly. One of my most used pots is a 2-quart cast aluminum IMUSA Dutch oven. This pot has cooked most of my food for many years, especially on hiking trips. A 2-quart pot is the perfect size for most needs of a single

A few aluminum cookware items can take you far.

Standard cast iron cookware can last many years.

person, and it's also the maximum size pot that can be taken on certain survival competition TV series such as *Alone* (food for thought in case you want to do a little training).

STAINLESS STEEL

Stainless steel is very prevalent in the camping world; the Pathfinder 10-inch stainless steel skillet has cooked many camping dishes for me over the years and I expect it'll continue to do so for years to come. Stainless steel is much heavier than titanium or aluminum but is durable and dependable, making

it perfect for use in the woods. Many modern camping cooking sets are made from stainless steel and come in a wide variety of sizes, from 8-ounce cups to huge 120-ounce bush pots. I have used the Pathfinder Woodland Chef series of bush pots for many years. This collection has everything you need to cook large meals for groups.

CAST IRON

Cast iron is fantastic for cooking. It distributes heat evenly and ensures you get close to an equal cooking temperature across the entire pot or

Enamelware can prevent some sticking but does not build up seasoning like cast iron.

skillet. A cast iron Dutch oven can handle most any task you can imagine, from frying fish to baking biscuits in an open fire. The only problem with cast iron is the weight. Although small, a 2-quart cast iron pot weighs more than 7 pounds, making it pretty impractical for hiking into the woods.

ENAMELWARE

This porcelain-coated steel pot is good for cooking stews and soups as well as boiling water over an open fire. Enamelware pots have many advantages: They don't have as many hot spots as titanium and aluminum, they're more stick-free than stainless steel and they're lighter than cast iron (roughly equivalent in weight to stainless steel). Enamelware does have a flaw when used in the camp setting, though, as it is possible for the porcelain to crack due to the extreme temperature of a campfire. If this happens, your food can become contaminated with porcelain chips. I recommended only using these pots and pans over coals on a grill (pg. 63) to more easily maintain a constant temperature.

Pots and pans are the vessels, whereas stoves, cranes, tripods, logs and fire holes are all tools that can be used with these metal containers to render food safe for consumption. But before we review how to build cooking tools from scratch, let's evaluate packable cooking items that could prove useful on a trip.

STOVES, OVENS AND GRILLS

While you may not be able to replicate quite the same level of convenience you're used to at home, these camping-friendly items can help you efficiently make a wider variety of meals than you might've imagined.

WOOD-BURNING STOVE

THESE STOVES OFFER a fantastic weight-to-value ratio—you can use them to cook food anywhere you go, and you don't have to carry the extra weight of fuel sources such as propane because they burn leaves, twigs, sticks and pine cones. Over the years, I have cooked an untold number of pots of beans and stews with a wood-burning stove. Some models can grill a steak if you're feeling extra ambitious. This variation of stove is also excellent for making coffee in the morning—all you have to do is throw in some leaves and twigs and your water will boil in no time.

Cooking on these stoves is very straightforward; light a fire like any other using the principles found in the Fire section, then just keep adding fuel as needed until your food has finished cooking. You can either open-roast food on a stick or use a pot like you would on a kitchen stove. This type of stove has multiple variations in different materials, including titanium and stainless steel, with varying assembly configurations. The one I have found to be the most useful is a folding stainless steel camp stove, which folds up like a book and is easily assembled. These particular stoves can help with "leave no trace" camping.

A good quality wood-burning stove can last many years.

Propane stoves can be used in conjunction with your campfire to cook multi-course meals.

PROPANE AND BUTANE STOVES

BETTER KNOWN AS expendable fuel stoves, these are commonly used by backpackers and hikers. Most people are already familiar with them. Propane stoves are great for boiling water to reconstitute freeze-dried foods and making tea and coffee. In my experience, though, propane burners are not ideal for cooking a pot of beans or a hearty stew from scratch in the woods because you expend more fuel (and therefore cash) doing something you can do for free over a simple fire. But this stove has a purpose and a place, and I don't want to discourage you from using one if that is your plan. Propane stoves are mainly used in environments where wood is scarce or nonexistent, leaving

no other alternative. If you're looking for a lightweight, all-in-one source to heat water and reconstitute food, a propane stove may be the perfect choice for you.

The propane comes in various sizes depending on your needs. For example, at the time of writing, the company MSR has three fuel bottle sizes: 3.9 ounce, 8 ounce and 16 ounce. The actual stove or burner portion can be found in different configurations made from stainless steel and titanium materials. With certain setups, you can boil water in less than a minute. If you're looking for a simple, packable stove that fits your budget or camping scenario, this stove could be all you need.

The hook on a bedroll stove is ideal for hanging a metal water bottle over the fire to purify water for drinking.

BEDROLL STOVE

STRAIGHTFORWARD, CONVENIENT AND relatively lightweight, this complete cooking system comes in a single bag that can be rolled up into your bedding (hence the name) and attached to the outside of your backpack. Similar to the adjustable pot crane (pg. 236) detailed later in this chapter, a bedroll stove allows your pot to be easily lowered and raised over the fire. The different accessories are held on with the weight of the pot or bottle.

The bedroll stove is easy to assemble; you simply attach three rods to each other and stick them into the ground next to the fire. Then, you place the grill or the pot and bottle hanger onto the rods. The weight of the pot will cause the rods to bend, but this is by design. As an added bonus, the waxed canvas pouch this stove comes with is perfect for keeping your gear from being covered in pesky soot.

BUSH POT OVEN

SOMETIMES WHEN YOU get into the woods, you want to be able to cook certain things like biscuits, fish or even a Cornish hen. Being able to improvise with what you have on hand is essential to primitive camping, and the bush pot is the king of versatility. Using a bush pot combined with the coals of your fire, you can make an improvised oven. The stainless steel Pathfinder 64-ounce bush pot comes with a small 4-by-4-inch grill that slides perfectly into the pot while lying on its side, making it perfect for baking biscuits. The lid creates an ideal oven door, allowing heat to stay inside. Because it's thinner, stainless steel will get hotter faster than cast iron, so you should keep a close eye on food to ensure it doesn't burn.

To prepare the bush pot oven:

Step 1 Move the coals to expose the dirt under the fire, then rake the coals under the sides and back of the pot.
Step 2 Place the pot where you just removed the coals.
Step 3 Put the food on the small grill, slide it inside the oven and put the lid on the pot.
Step 4 Scrape a small amount of coals around the sides and back of the pot.

As your food cooks, use the pliers on your multi-tool to remove the lid to check progress. Make sure you wear gloves to protect your fingers from burns. If the oven is not cooking as fast as you would like, add more coals to the sides and back of the pot.

The Pathfinder allows you to lock the bale handle in place to prevent spilling.

DUTCH OVEN

THE SAME PRINCIPLE used with the bush pot can be used with a cast iron Dutch oven. I would not recommend doing this setup with an aluminum Dutch oven because it could melt the aluminum (I learned this the hard way). A cast iron Dutch oven is basically the multi-tool of the camp kitchen. When placed on a bed of coals, a large Dutch oven can be used to bake biscuits and roast chickens or armadillos, while a smaller 8-inch cast iron Dutch oven can cook everything from eggs in the morning to pots of chili in the evening. The lid of a Dutch oven can even be turned upside down and placed over coals to be used as a griddle or hot plate to cook sausage, fish, vegetables and even pancakes. Most Dutch ovens designed for camping have legs for use in the campfire, a deep lip on the lid for placing coals on top and a bale to hang the pot on a tripod or hook. If you find a cast iron Dutch oven that doesn't have these features, it is intended for home use on a regular gas or electric stove.

To make Dutch oven biscuits:

Step 1 Grease the bottom and sides of the pot with a few squirts of oil.
Step 2 Place biscuits inside the oven and put the lid on. Rake the coals in the same manner as with the bush pot oven and place the Dutch oven on the coals.
Step 3 Place coals on top of the lid. The smaller the pot, the fewer coals you'll need to reach a higher temperature.

> ## QUICK TIP
> **This method can also be used to roast meat in a Dutch oven.**

A Dutch oven can also make anything from pizzas to banana bread to nachos.

PACKABLE GRILLS

THERE ARE MANY portable grills on the market today, from the colossal cowboy-style grills you need a truck to transport to tiny 6-by-6-inch fold-up grills that fit in a backpack. Naturally, a smaller, packable grill is the more convenient option to carry. These grills weigh roughly the same amount as a wood-burning or biomass stove and can also be used in conjunction with the Dakota fire hole (pg. 244). A small grill placed over a good bed of coals can cook any food and boil water for drinking. Used in the same manner as a kitchen stove at home, it can also accommodate a skillet for sausage and powdered eggs or a pot for beans or stew. Just treat it like you were throwing a Fourth of July barbecue!

To cook with a packable grill:

Step 1 Start a fire with more fuel than you think you need.
Step 2 Let the fire burn down to a hot bed of coals.
Step 3 Rake some coals into your cooking area and place your grill/grate over the coals.

These coals will burn for a relatively long time, and you can continue to fuel the fire behind the grill and rake more coals under the grill as needed. To increase the temperature, add more coals (and remove coals to reduce the temperature). Treat it like you would a barbecue pit: When you use a charcoal grill, you're cooking on coals; you're ready to grill once the fire burns down and the briquettes turn white. The same concept should be applied to cooking over a campfire with a portable grill. Keep an eye out for flare-ups and manage them as necessary.

Another way to use a small portable grill is to dig a hole smaller than the width of the grill, allowing the legs to rest on each side of the hole. Making the spot no more than 2 inches deep will allow you to keep oxygen flowing to the fire and give you the same benefit as a wood-burning stove without the extra weight.

BRINGING A BIGGER GRILL

While you may not be hiking deep into the woods with a larger grill, you can bring one if you're using some conveyance like an ATV or boat to get to your campsite. I routinely use a boat to take me miles downriver to a secluded spot where I set up a primitive camp. Using the boat, I can transport oversized items, such as a large grill, making my camp kitchen perfect for cooking anything I can imagine.

PRIMITIVE COOKING TOOLS AND METHODS

Once you've gotten comfortable cooking with convenient items such as stoves and grills in the wild, you can elevate your camp kitchen with some ingenious tools and methods. You just need a willingness to think outside the box and a few good sticks.

NOTCHES

BEFORE YOU CAN start making cooking tools out of sticks, you must know how to make notches. Notches allow you to hang, secure, affix and join wooden pieces. There are various notches, all with unique purposes, from making trap triggers to pot hangers for cooking. Notches are easily made with your knife or folding saw on green wood and become more difficult with dead wood. As a bonus, making a notch is the test of a good knife and will let you know if your favorite blade is too thick or dull.

Essentially, notches are to cooking tools what knots are to cordage.

"V" NOTCH

THE "V" NOTCH is used on pot cranes to suspend your pot over a fire and is the simplest notch to make.

Step 1 Roughly 1-1 ½ inches from the end of your stick, drive your knife in at a 45-degree angle. Leave a cut to your desired depth (typically no more than half the thickness of the stick).

Step 2 Repeat the same process in the opposite direction, removing the material between the two cuts to create a "V" shape.

> ### QUICK TIP
> **Notches can also be made with a folding saw.**

The "V" should be apparent from either side of the stick.

LOG CABIN NOTCH

ALSO KNOWN AS the square notch, these notches were used on a large scale to make log cabins throughout history and are still used today.

Step 1 Using your knife or saw, make two perpendicular cuts into the stick to your desired depth (typically no more than half the thickness of the stick).
Step 2 Remove the material between the two cuts, leaving a square-shaped notch.

A NOTCH ABOVE THE REST

Log cabin notches were also used to assemble some primitive weapons, such as the Apache throwing star. This weapon is made from two sticks of equal length lashed together thanks to log cabin notches cut into the middle of both sticks. The ends of each shaft were then sharpened to a point, making the Apache star effective for hunting small game such as rabbits and squirrels.

Clear out the space between cuts until the sides of the square appear flat.

POT HOOK NOTCH

THE POT HOOK notch is used to hang a pot over a fire.

Step 1 Roughly 1½ inches from the bottom of your stick, make an X by holding your blade 45 degrees to your stick on each side. Using a mallet, baton the back of your blade into the wood until you are halfway through.
Step 2 Carve out the top three sections of the X, leaving the bottom section.
Step 3 Your finished notch should look like an eagle's beak.

Carve slowly to avoid going too deep.

A well-made pot hanger can support plenty of weight.

Avoid cooking over direct flames as this can cover your pots with soot and burn your food.

POT CRANE

A POT CRANE IS a handy device that elevates your pot above the fire. I have used this method hundreds of times when camping, and it has never failed me. It can be used in various ways and made from different materials, but for our purposes, you'll simply need three sticks.

Stick 1 (Y Branch) Find a forked stick or Y branch. It can vary in length depending on your fire size and the softness of the ground, but I typically use one between 12 and 24 inches long. This Y branch is going to elevate your pot crane above the fire. The bigger or hotter the fire, the longer your Y branch should be.

Stick 2 (Crane) You'll need a long stick between 4 and 6 feet for the actual crane. At the end of the stick, carve either a "V" notch or log cabin notch. This notch will hold the bale of your pot above the fire.

Stick 3 (Seven Branch) The last stick is a seven branch, meaning it is an upside-down Y, but one side is cut short and the other is left long. It should resemble the number seven.

LID LIFTER

One problem you may run into when cooking over fire is removing the lid of a pot. To bushcraft an improvised lid lifter, you can carve a 45-degree flat angle on the end of a stick with a log cabin notch approximately 1 inch from the tip. The angle should fit flat against the lid while the log cabin notch fits under the lid's handle, allowing you to lift the lid.

QUICK TIP

Open fire roasting can be done with the same setup; just sharpen the stick's end to a point rather than carving a notch and impale your food on it.

The long end of this stick will be carved to a point and driven into the ground at the end of your pot crane to provide stability.

Step 1 Sharpen the end of the Y branch to a point and drive it into the ground about 12 inches away from the edge of your fire.

NOTE: Use the side of the stick that is the central part of the branch to drive into the ground. If you hit the portion that grew from the shaft of the main branch making the Y, it will break off.

Step 2 Take your pot crane stick and position the notch upward and align the end of the stick so your pot will hang over the center of your fire. The pot does not have to be in the center of the fire if cooking over open coals but should be if boiling water.

Step 3 Drive the seven branch into the ground at the end of your pot crane. This will hold the pot crane down and keep it stable no matter how much liquid you put into the pot.

NOTE: As stated above, the length of your Y branch and seven branch will depend on the soil quality you are pounding it into. You must drive it deeper into the ground if dealing with very sandy soil.

ADJUSTABLE POT CRANE

IN RECENT YEARS, I have started using an adjustable pot crane or friction pot crane. This particular pot crane also only requires three sticks. **NOTE:** To better help the friction of this appliance, leave the bark on all three sticks.

Stick 1 (Central Pole) The main branch, called the central pole, should be about 1½ to 2 inches in diameter and about 4 feet long.
Stick 2 (Y Branch) Find a Y branch roughly 1 to 1½ inches in diameter and 3 feet long (I tend to use a branch that is slightly curved and then face the curve up).
Stick 3 (Stop Block) You will need a short stick 8 to 10 inches long called a stop block. The stop block should be the same diameter as your central pole.

Step 1 Sharpen the end of your central pole and drive it into the ground; it must be deep enough to hold the weight of a couple of gallons of water. Use another large stick or the butt of your axe to hammer it into the ground.
Step 2 With the curve of your Y branch facing up, carve a "V" notch or a log cabin notch for the bale of your pot approximately two finger lengths from the end.
Step 3 Insert the central pole into the Y branch and use your knife to make a reference mark on each side of the Y branch. These marks will be where you lash the stop block to the Y branch.
Step 4 Using a jam knot (pg. 31), lash the stop block to and on top of the Y branch on the marks, then finish it off with a clove hitch (pg. 29).
Step 5 Place the newly created arm onto your central pole. The stop block should be tight against the main branch but still loose enough so that it will allow you to raise and lower the arm on the central pole.

NOTE: The arm will sag slightly, but that's OK. Just don't let it droop so low that the pot is in the fire—if this happens, your main arm is too long or too thin.

The finished product should adjust with ease while remaining tightly bound.

TRIPOD

TRIPODS HAVE BEEN used to cook for centuries. They are easy to make and use, and they have multiple uses beyond cooking, making them a versatile item to keep around camp.

Step 1 Find long, sturdy sticks or branches. Cut into three poles of equal length and lay them next to each other on the ground. Make a loop with your bank line or paracord using an overhand loop knot. Place the loop around the end of the sticks, ensuring it's not excessively tight.

Step 2 Flip the middle pole 180 degrees in order to tighten the loop onto the sticks.

Step 3 Stand the tripod up and spread the legs out.

USING THE TRIPOD

Place your tripod over the fire or where you intend to start your fire.

Cut a length of bank line and make an overhand loop knot slightly larger than the combined diameter of your poles on the tripod. Place this loop over the center pole and slide it down until it rests where the tripod is lashed together. Let the string dangle down toward where the fire will be.

Make a toggle from a stick slightly larger than the width of the bail (handle) on your pot. Secure the toggle to the string with a lark's head or clove hitch (pg. 29), considering how deep your pot is so that it will hang over the fire and not in it.

To control the temperature while cooking, move the tripod legs in or out to raise the pot up or down, or make an adjustable pot hanger.

CHEAP TRIPOD BOARD

A tripod board is relatively lightweight and makes your tripod setup extremely quick without the need for cordage. Usually cut into a triangle shape with three large corner holes and one smaller center hole, this piece of metal provides support via tension once the tripod legs are placed in the corner holes. The center hole is for an adjustable chain or trammel. A trammel is an adjustable pot hook traditionally used for a fireplace or crane that was long ago adapted for use with tripod systems. Modern tripod boards usually come with a chain and hook, which can be used to adjust the height of your pot. This setup is effortless and can be found online for low prices.

If you're not feeling enough tension, re-tie the loop slightly tighter.

Tripods are great for making smoked fish, which goes well with beans and rice.

TRIPOD SMOKER

WHEN A FIRE lacks oxygen to burn fuel or logs completely, it gives off tiny particles that, when combined in large enough quantities, are visible as smoke. Smoking your food helps preserve it for later use by reducing the moisture content and protecting it from bacteria. The smoke also augments the flavor, especially when combined with a bit of salt and pepper. The trick to smoking is to make a low-temperature fire (which may sound like an absurd concept). You want some heat, but you also want to capture the smoke.

Step 1 Use the tripod you made for cooking or create another one. Make shelves on the tripod to place your food by lashing sticks to each leg and then lashing sticks across those until it resembles a grill. Make as many shelves as you need for the amount of food you will be smoking.

Step 2 To trap the smoke, wrap your tripod with a sheet or tarp. If you do not have a sheet or tarp, this can be done with spruce boughs, pine branches or large chunks of bark from dead trees. To ensure your fire does not burn a hole through your sheet or tarp, dig a hole 12 inches deep where the fire will be.

NOTE: You can stand poles, sticks or large chunks of tree bark in a teepee shape to enclose your tripod.

The adjustable pot hanger is a length of cordage that has loop knots on both ends.

1. Attach one loop to the center pole on the top of the tripod and feed the bottom loop through the bale of your pot.

QUICK TIP

If you bring a roll of 26 gauge floral wire, you can hang fish by the tail inside your smoker.

2. Bring the overhand loop knot up to the string and feed the string through the loop and insert a toggle. This toggle will allow you to raise and lower your pot over the fire without moving the tripod to adjust your cooking temperature.

WHICH WOOD WORKS BEST

I typically use oak or hickory wood to get a good flavor when smoking meat. Pecan, wild cherry or any nut-bearing tree are all suitable for smoking as well, and I have even used magnolia successfully. Do not use spruce, fir, sycamore, elm, cypress, eastern cedar, eucalyptus, amber, redwood, sassafras or any species of pine trees. These highly resinous trees contain oils that can cause ill health effects.

OPEN-FIRE ROASTING

THIS COOKING METHOD has been used since the early days of civilization and does not require a pot. Open-fire roasting is my favorite way to cook quail and rabbit when camping. When using this method, you want to avoid cooking directly over the fire—instead, your pot or spit should be in front of or off to the side. As with most open-fire cooking, you want to wait for the fire to die down, then rake the coals to where the cooking will take place. You can also place what you want to roast on a rock near the fire in an area with large stones. Here are a few different open-fire roasting methods.

SPIT-ROASTING

Spit-roasting was the primary means of cooking for soldiers during the Civil War, and it remains a very useful method for primitive campers today. Additionally, you can hang multiple pots on the spit as you're roasting so you can cook multiple dishes at once.

Step 1 Select two Y branches thick enough to support the weight of whatever you will be cooking with (meat, hanging pots, etc.).
Step 2 For the spit, select a stick wider than your fire area so that it can rest on both Y branches (this will be what you roast your meat on or hang your pots from).
Step 3 Sharpen the end of each Y branch to a point. Drive one branch into the ground 8 inches away from your fire, then do the same on the opposite side.
Step 4 If you plan to roast meat, remove the bark from your long stick.
Step 5 Place your long stick across the fire so that it rests on each Y branch.

POT CRANE ROASTING

This roasting method involves a modified pot crane (pg. 235).

Step 1 Select a green sapling 4 to 6 feet in length. Shave the bark off the sapling and sharpen the end to a point. Insert the point into the center of the meat.
Step 2 As demonstrated on pg. 235, drive a Y branch into the ground and lay your roasting stick against it.
Step 3 For stability, place a seven branch

CHIPS OFF THE OLD BLOCK

A trick my dad taught me when I was younger was to make smoking wood into chips with an axe.

Use your axe or hatchet to cut chips (more than you think you will need) from your smoking wood. The size of the chips does not matter.

Soak the chips in water for about an hour before you smoke your food. Soaking the chips will allow them to smoke better and not burn up quickly but rather burn slowly as the water evaporates.

Throw a few handfuls of chips on the fire. This helps with generating smoke, especially on a smaller fire.

Cutting your smoking wood into large chunks also helps with the smoking process. A 2- to 3-inch thick log can be cut into 4 to 6 inch chunks and thrown onto the fire to create plenty of smoke. Food can be hung near the fire without being in a smoker and still absorb full wood-fire flavor. I have suspended fish from a tripod without wrapping the tripod with a sheet or tarp and still enjoyed fully cooked, smoky, flavorful fish.

or something heavy like a rock or log on the end of the stick, suspending the meat over the heat. The butt end of the stick can even be sharpened and shoved into the ground without using anything else to hold it down.

Step 4 Rotate the stick often, allowing the meat to cook evenly and thoroughly.

NOTE: You can also use a pot for this setup.

Whether roasting with a spit or pot crane, an open fire provides flavor and efficiency.

DAKOTA FIRE HOLE

THE DAKOTA FIRE hole is named after the Native American tribe who used it while stalking bison for two reasons: to protect their fires from the constant wind on the plains and to keep the prairie from catching fire. This fire is extremely hot, nearly smokeless and world-renowned as the ultimate cooking fire as highlighted in books including *The Official U.S. Army Survival Handbook*. As mentioned on pg. 241, smoke results from the incomplete burning of organic matter or fuel. This fire, however, gets enough oxygen to reach temperatures hot enough to burn practically all the fuel, leaving only carbon dioxide and water.

The Dakota fire hole is a great option when cooking in the woods because it can operate on smaller amounts of fuel, burn hotter than a regular campfire and is easily controlled so you do not have to worry as much about burning the forest down.

NOTE: This fire will not work next to water because when you dig your holes, they could backfill with the water source and extinguish your fire. It does not work well with very sandy soil either because the earth tends to collapse, extinguishing your fire.

Step 1 Dig a hole up to 14 inches in diameter and approximately 12 to 14

The Dakota fire hole can function as a primitive grill or stove, depending on your needs.

will be. This will continue to allow an upward draft, pulling more oxygen into the fire.

inches deep.

Step 2 About 10 to 12 inches away from the first, dig a second hole 8 to 10 inches in diameter. Try to dig at an angle toward the first hole.

Step 3 Use a stick to dig a tunnel from the second hole to the bottom of the first hole. Remove all the dirt that was displaced.

Step 4 Start a fire as you usually would, loading all the material in the first hole.

Step 5 To cook, lay a few strong sticks across the hole, allowing your pot to hover above the hole where the fire

To use the Dakota fire hole as a stove, set your grill over the hole instead of laying sticks across the opening. Typically you would use this method with a pot or skillet. When cooking with the Dakota fire hole, you will be practically cooking over open flames, not coals. This method is like cooking with a gas stove on high at home, and it will be harder to control the temperature until you let the flames die down. Remember that the Dakota fire hole will burn much hotter than another fire of similar size. Using a grill gives you more room to add fuel to the fire without picking the grill up and moving it constantly, and it will also give you more temperature control since the pot is raised higher above the fire.

ADDITIONAL ITEMS

WHILE NOT ALWAYS essential, these items can make your campfire cooking experience even more efficient and enjoyable.

ALUMINUM FOIL

Aluminum foil is a fantastic item to have on hand for cooking. Place your fresh catch of the day with some vegetables on the foil doubled over, give it a few squirts of oil and season it with salt and pepper. Fold both sides up, roll them down together, then roll the ends toward the middle. Place the package near the coals of your fire with the fold side facing up, then either kick back and watch the fire or go to tend to some camp chores for 20 minutes. Then, flip the package over and 20 to 30 minutes later, you'll have an entire dish ready to eat. This method is perfect for potatoes and other veggies like bell peppers, onions and mushrooms and convenient for cooking them while something else is on the grill or in the Dutch oven.

Aluminum foil can also be used to clean your pots and pans after you cook. Wad up a small ball and use it as a scrubber pad to remove stubborn, stuck-on food. For the really stuck food (such as burnt food), boil a little water in the pot, pour it out and then use the aluminum foil to scrub the pan.

UTENSILS

There are many variations of camp

A survival spork eliminates the need to pack both a spoon and a fork.

Bushcraft tongs can sometimes be made from leftover materials gathered to make another cooking tool.

BUSHCRAFT TONGS

Sometimes you may need to pick something up out of hot coals, such as a metal container when making charcloth or a potato wrapped in aluminum foil. When leather gloves just won't cut it, you can make a pair of tongs.

Step 1 Find a green wood Y branch approximately 18 to 24 inches long.
Step 2 Find another green wood branch and cut a straight stick the same length and diameter as the Y branch.
Step 3 Place the Y branch at the base of the item you want to remove from the fire. Now place the straight stick through the Y branch and over the item you want to extract from the fire. Squeeze them together and lift the object out.

CAMPING POT HOLDER

I found a pot holder in a camping store that changed how I remove pots from fire and even changed how I hold metal bowls while eating hot foods. These little grippers fit around the lip of the pot or cup you want to lift off the fire. They work like pliers and get tighter the harder you squeeze them. They also have high-temperature rubber on the lip to prevent you from bending and scoring your metal pots.

utensils on the market today, from plastic sporks and knives to stainless steel dual-sided spoons and forks to incredibly lightweight titanium utensils. There are folding spoons and forks that look like giant Swiss Army knives and even something called the survival spork, which has a steak knife and ferro rod built in. It's easy to forget eating utensils when packing for a trip, which is why you should always keep one set in your cookware bag and another in your food bag. This way, you won't have to carve your own fork or spoon when you're in the woods.

If you forget a spatula, you can easily carve one from green non-resinous softwood—all you need is a relatively wide stick carved flat on both sides and a handle whittled down to your preferred size. This spatula can also be used to clean your cast iron pot if food gets stuck.

As for knives, you should bring more than one on your trip anyway. If you cut raw meat with it, just ensure your knife is thoroughly cleaned before cutting prepared food.

The pot holder allows you to safely pick up hot items off the fire.

INDEX

ACKNOWLEDGMENTS

I WANT TO EXPRESS MY DEEPEST GRATITUDE and appreciation to my incredible wife, Nicole. Her steadfast support, boundless encouragement and unwavering belief in me have been the cornerstone of this book's existence. Nicole, you have been my rock throughout this entire journey. Your patience, understanding and willingness to listen to my countless camping stories and ideas have been nothing short of remarkable. Your constant reassurance and loving presence propel me forward, even in moments when self-doubt threatens to hold me back. I am eternally grateful for you in my life, not only as my wife but as my best friend and the driving force behind all my crazy endeavors. This book would not have been possible without you by my side. Your support has transformed my camping adventures into a written tale, and for that I am forever indebted to you.

Thank you to my mom, Cheryl, for helping me with so many of the ideas in this book, especially in the Food section. And to my brother, Aaron; many of the stories in this book are based on our trips, and I can't wait to see where we go next! Thanks to my sons, Logan and Mason (you too, Anna Grace), extended family, friends and the staff at Media Lab Books. I couldn't have done this without all of your support.

Most importantly, thank you Jesus for transforming me from a broken man into a completely renewed individual and taking me from a path of self-destruction to a road with a future. In Matthew 11:28, Jesus said, "Come to me, all who labor and are heavy laden, and I will give you rest." I'll tell you: If you haven't tried it, don't knock it! If I can change from who I used to be to who I am now, so can you!

Last but not least, I sincerely appreciate every Speir Outdoors community member. As I typically say at the end of my videos, follow Jesus and everything else will fall into place. I will see you next time. God bless you!

ABOUT THE AUTHOR

CHRIS SPEIR IS THE FOUNDER OF SPEIR OUTDOORS, the hugely popular online community devoted to primitive camping and survival. Speir has spent his entire life camping, hunting and fishing. In that time, he has mastered the art of survival in the wilderness with minimal resources and established Speir Outdoors to teach those skills to others. Chris is also a professional wildlife photographer. He lives in southern Mississippi.

You can follow all of Chris's outdoor adventures online at *speiroutdoors.com* or on YouTube, Instagram, TikTok, Facebook and Pinterest @speiroutdoors.

Media Lab Books
For inquiries, call 646-449-8614

Copyright 2024 Chris Speir

Published by Topix Media Lab
14 Wall Street, Suite 3C
New York, NY 10005

Printed in China

ISBN-13: 978-1-956403-58-9
ISBN-10: 1-956403-58-2

CEO Tony Romando

Vice President & Publisher Phil Sexton
Senior Vice President of Sales & New Markets Tom Mifsud
Vice President of Retail Sales & Logistics Linda Greenblatt
Chief Financial Officer Vandana Patel
Vice President of Manufacturing & Distribution Nancy Puskuldjian
Digital Marketing & Strategy Manager Elyse Gregov

Chief Content Officer Jeff Ashworth
Senior Acquisitions Editor Noreen Henson
Creative Director Susan Dazzo
Photo Director Dave Weiss
Executive Editor Tim Baker
Managing Editor Tara Sherman

Content Editor Trevor Courneen
Content Designer Glen Karpowich
Associate Editor Juliana Sharaf
Designers Alyssa Bredin Quirós, Mikio Sakai
Copy Editor & Fact Checker Madeline Raynor
Assistant Photo Editor Jenna Addesso
Assistant Managing Editor Claudia Acevedo

Photographs by Chris Speir
Additional art: Shutterstock

Indexing by Meridith Murray

1C-J23-1